Food
SELF-SUFFICIENCY

Visit our website at www.skyhorsepublishing.com.

10 9 8 7 6 5 4 3 2 1

Library of Congress Cataloging-in-Publication Data is available on file.

Cover design by David Ter-Avanesyan
Cover image by iStock, Shutterstock, and Frédéric Marre/RUSTICA

Print ISBN: 978-1-5107-6821-5
Ebook ISBN: 978-1-5107-7048-5

Printed in China

Food SELF-SUFFICIENCY

Basic Permaculture Techniques for Vegetable Gardening, Keeping Chickens, Raising Bees, and More

Robert Elger

English translation by Grace McQuillan

Skyhorse Publishing

Contents

6 CULTIVATING YOUR GARDEN AND STARTING SEEDLINGS

7 KEEPING CHICKENS

8 BEEKEEPING

9 GRAIN PRODUCTION

10 HARVEST

11 STORING AND PRESERVING YOUR HARVEST

12 GARDEN CALENDAR FOR A SELF-SUFFICIENT YEAR

13 PERMACULTURE AND AUTONOMY

Foreword

Being independent is all about being able to meet your own needs, and, more precisely, it's about having within reach the things you need to lead a full life. When we talk about independence in the broad sense, we are primarily concerned with our intellectual, emotional, and social lives. On a more practical level, though, being independent is also about producing all—or at least a large part—of our personal food supply.

On the way to food self-sufficiency

From time immemorial, the great provider of family food has been the bit of earth surrounding the home. Not so very long ago, vegetables from the garden, fruit from the orchard, eggs from the chicken coop, and honey from beehives made up a significant portion of the food we consumed. A few dozen yards at most was all that separated the place where food was produced from the kitchen where it was prepared and consumed. One would be hard-pressed to create a shorter food supply chain! While the garden's role has diminished since the end of World War II, it has never completely disappeared, especially in rural areas. In fact, it is making a comeback, and now many of us are turning our land into our very own grocery stores.

How much land do I need?

Any new project requires having certain resources in place. As a rule, the farther your home is from urban areas the more space you will have available to cultivate. If your goal is to grow food for family consumption, 700 square yards (less than ¼ acre) of land is enough to give you vegetables, herbs, most fruits, eggs, and even honey since two or three hives won't take up very much room. If you want to enlarge your food supply and include grains and protein crops as well, aim for around half an acre. That said, a plot of 240 to 360 square yards is nothing to laugh at, and, as this book will show you, that's more than enough land to give you access to fresh produce all year long.

Gardening requires many different skills . . .

While it may appear simple, managing a garden requires knowledge in a variety of areas. To make your project a success, you'll have to take turns being—at the very least!—a botanist, meteorologist, agronomist, truck farmer, nurseryman, tree grower, poultry breeder, and a beekeeper. Studying all of these fields ahead of time—as you are doing by reading this book—will help you avoid quite a few blunders and equip you to make decisions more easily. In the long term, as experience has shown, your knowledge and know-how are what will make the real difference.

. . . and the right tools

Taking your life and environment into your own hands means you'll have to get those hands dirty. Will you have to do everything yourself? Maybe not, but there's a lot you can do. With what? Tools, of course! And those tools will become an invaluable part of your self-sufficiency. Get yourself started with a range of basic tools and a few multipurpose tools that are always in a handyman's toolbox—a hammer, pliers, and a few different screwdrivers and saws—and add to it over time depending on your needs. A small set of electric tools is also practical and should include a drill and, potentially, a jigsaw or circular saw. You may even decide to invest in a welding machine. Finally, you will need a set of gardening hand tools including pruning shears, a spade, a broadfork and spading fork, cultivators and hooks, a rake, a weeding hoe, and a bucket and trowel; these will become indispensable. Whether you're buying large or hand-size tools, prioritize solidity, effectiveness, and simplicity. If you protect them from the weather and take care of them, they will last you years. The handle is the part that usually breaks first, but these days you can find fiberglass handles that are as durable as metal.

Share!

Becoming independent doesn't mean cutting yourself off from other people. Social and relational isolation—as we all know—is harmful to our intellectual and emotional equilibrium and even to our physical health. True self-sufficiency happens when we relate to others in a variety of ways, including bartering and giving gifts. All gardens, not just communal ones, are places of exchange. Anything can be shared—seeds, young plants, straw, eggs—because one person's surplus might be exactly what someone else needs, and vice versa.

Robert Elger

1
FOOD SELF-SUFFICIENCY

There may be more to being self-reliant than having an independent source of food, but the two are closely linked. "You are what you eat," as the popular saying goes. In his book *Appetites for Thought: Philosophers and Food*, Michel Onfray says essentially the same thing: by examining the contents of their plates, we are able to understand who Diogenes, Kant, Rousseau, Nietzsche, and Sartre really were. Producing your own vegetables, herbs, and fruit—maybe even grains and honey, too—will provide you with just about all the food you need.

Vegetables

There are roughly sixty vegetable species commonly cultivated in gardens today, and around one hundred others that are lesser known but fairly easy to grow. All of these vegetables exist in a sometimes staggering number of varieties, which only further broadens the range of options available to

you. Their harvest is usually limited to a single growing season, but the choice of variety can sometimes extend the season for each crop. You will find, for example, lettuce varieties for spring, summer, fall, and winter; cabbage varieties for summer, fall, and winter; varieties of frisée and escarole that grow in summer or fall; and even leek varieties that can be harvested in fall and winter.

Depending on the vegetable and what part of it is being harvested—leaves, fruit, roots, shoots, flowers, or seeds—harvest takes place in either spring, summer, fall, or winter. The growing season for spring radishes, for instance, rarely extends beyond two months, but leeks and parsnips can be left in the ground for an entire year. Annual vegetables complete a cycle every year that takes them from germination to the creation of new seeds. Biennials, on the other hand, develop during the first year and produce seeds the second year while perennial vegetables live for several years—up to fifteen years or more in the case of asparagus and rhubarb.

In any case, it's always a good idea to diversify your crops. But remember: while not enough diversity can weaken your garden's agricultural potential and limit your possibilities in the kitchen, too much diversification is unmanageable, especially if you are producing your own seeds. The key is finding the right balance. So, which vegetables should you grow? The answer is simple: grow the ones you enjoy and hope to see on your table.

Leaf vegetables

Leaf vegetables—plants harvested for their leaves, in other words—wilt after only a short time, but because they can be used in the kitchen immediately after being picked, this should not pose a problem for family gardens. These crops grow in abundance from spring through fall, but hardier varieties can stay in your garden all winter. Mild winters in some places have extended the harvest of many fall vegetables like celery, frisée, and escarole until the following spring. Endives and a variety of other chicories can also be force-grown indoors and will invite themselves to the table from November to April.

Spring offers you the chance to harvest, among other things, saltbush, red cabbage, perennial kale, garlic mustard, Good-King-Henry, sorrel, and Turkish arugula, which conveniently starts growing vigorously in late winter. Summer is the time to harvest New Zealand spinach, the many varieties of amaranth, watercress, oyster leaf with its

curious salty flavor, buck's-horn plantain (*Plantago coronopus*), edible chrysanthemum, and the flavorful baby sun rose (*Aptenia cordifolia,* now known as *Mesembryanthemum cordifolium*). Land cress can be harvested in the fall (its growing season extends into the heart of winter) along with cardoon and mustard greens.

Turkish arugula is sometimes called Turkish warty-cabbage and can be harvested beginning in the month of February.

→ AVAILABILITY OF MAJOR LEAF VEGETABLES

Keep in mind that growing seasons vary according to your region. This chart is based on USDA hardiness zones 6–7, but because there can be a great deal of variation even within each zone, check with neighbors or your local agricultural extension office for information specific to your area.

	J	F	M	A	M	J	J	A	S	O	N	D
Arugula	▨	▨	▨	▨	▨	▨				▨	▨	▨
Bok choy									▨	▨	▨	
Brussels sprouts (depending on variety)	▨	▨	▨								▨	▨
Cabbage (depending on variety)							▨	▨		▨	▨	▨
Celery								▨	▨	▨	▨	
Chard	▨	▨				▨	▨	▨			▨	▨
Dandelion			▨	▨	▨							
Endive (forced)	▨	▨								▨	▨	▨
Escarole, summer and fall						▨	▨	▨	▨	▨	▨	
Frisée, summer and fall						▨	▨	▨	▨	▨	▨	
Head lettuce, fall									▨	▨	▨	
Head lettuce, spring					▨	▨						
Head lettuce, summer							▨	▨				
Head lettuce, winter		▨	▨									
Kale	▨	▨	▨	▨							▨	▨
Mâche	▨	▨									▨	▨
Miner's lettuce	▨	▨										▨
Napa cabbage	▨										▨	▨
Purslane						▨	▨	▨				
Radicchio (depending on variety)	▨	▨							▨	▨	▨	
Red cabbage									▨	▨	▨	
Savoy cabbage		▨	▨							▨	▨	
Sorrel				▨	▨	▨						
Spinach	▨	▨		▨	▨						▨	▨
Various Asian cabbages					▨				▨	▨	▨	
Wild chicory									▨	▨	▨	▨

▨ Harvest

Stem vegetables

The most well-known stem vegetable, the leek, has a long white barrel that is partially buried in the soil with blue-green upper leaves. Kohlrabi and fennel also have edible stems. In the case of kohlrabi, the stem swells at the end of the growing season to form a spherical or conical pseudo-root about four inches (ten centimeters) in diameter. In the fennel plant, the base of the leaves expands to form an edible faux bulb.

The perpetual leek is less widespread than the common leek and also grows in a very different manner. Though usually cultivated as a biennial, it is a perennial plant, and its cloves are planted in summer to produce a harvest all winter long. Sea kale, an even more unusual stem vegetable, is an extremely hardy and perennial cabbage relative that can survive in the same place for several years. Its young shoots, forced or not, can be harvested beginning in February. Hops are traditionally grown for their highly aromatic female cones, but their particularly tasty young shoots also merit a place in the garden.

HARVESTING YOUNG SHOOTS

A number of Asian cabbages including mizuna, komatsuna, and kailaan are sown in either February or September and then picked as young shoots. Their rapid growth and flexibility in terms of temperature—they germinate and grow anywhere above 45°F (8°C)—make them prized garden vegetables in both spring and fall.

→ AVAILABILITY OF MAJOR STEM VEGETABLES

Keep in mind that growing seasons vary according to your region. This chart is based on USDA hardiness zones 6–7, but because there can be a great deal of variation even within each zone, check with neighbors or your local agricultural extension office for information specific to your area.

	J	F	M	A	M	J	J	A	S	O	N	D
Asparagus				▓	▓							
Fennel (depending on planting time)						▓	▓	▓	▓			
Kohlrabi (depending on planting time)						▓	▓		▓			
Leek (depending on variety)	▓	▓	▓	▓				▓	▓	▓	▓	▓

 Harvest

Fruiting vegetables

Fruiting vegetables are the kings of the kitchen garden in summer and fall. Tomatoes, eggplants, and peppers are ready to eat as soon as they are picked, and squash is harvested before the harsh weather and can be stored somewhere cool and dry for months—in some cases until spring.

In addition to these more popular species, there are other less common fruiting vegetables that have found their way into our gardens. Chayote is a climbing gourd vine that ripens in the fall and produces fruits that resemble large pears. The fig-leaf gourd—while it doesn't taste like one—looks just like a freshly picked watermelon! The vila-vila, tomatillo, and pepino plants grow like tomatoes, but the tamarillo is a shrub that is highly frost-sensitive and does best in a pot away from winter cold, much like other decorative Mediterranean plants like oleander and angel's trumpets. Kitchen gardens in areas with mild winters can sustain a variety of African eggplants like *Solanum macrocarpon* and *Solanum aethiopicum*. The Armenian cucumber, Sikkim cucumber, cucamelon, kiwano, and caigua can all thrive alongside more common cucumber varieties. The yardlong bean develops long cylindrical pods that give the plant its name, and okra is a flowering plant in the same family as hibiscus whose fruit is used to thicken and flavor sauces. The rat-tail radish is a curious plant in the Brassicaceae family whose fleshy seedpods have a spicy flavor.

Also known as horned cucumber, the kiwano is an interesting member of the Cucurbitaceae family found in Africa. Its fruity flavor is reminiscent of melon, banana, and kiwi.

13

→ AVAILABILITY OF MAJOR FRUITING VEGETABLES

Keep in mind that growing seasons vary according to your region. This chart is based on USDA hardiness zones 6–7, but because there can be a great deal of variation even within each zone, check with neighbors or your local agricultural extension office for information specific to your area.

	J	F	M	A	M	J	J	A	S	O	N	D
Bush beans							■	■	■			
Cucumber						■	■	■				
Eggplant							■	■	■			
Melon and watermelon								■	■			
Pepper							■	■				
Physalis peruviana									■	■	■	
Sweet corn								■	■			
Tomato							■	■	■			
Turban squash, red kuri squash, and pumpkin	░	░							■	■	░	░
Winter squash	░	░	░	░					■	■	░	░
Zucchini and pattypan squash						■	■	■	■			

■ Harvest
░ Storage

The Ethiopian eggplant (*Solanum aethiopicum*) is an African Solanaceae variety that resembles a tomato.

Flower vegetables

Flower vegetables are grown for their young buds and are harvested before they have fully opened.

Broccoli rabe and sprouting broccoli are close relatives of Calabrese broccoli. Their inflorescences (or buds) are smaller, but their ability to resist cold temperatures extends their harvest until early winter and early spring, respectively.

The artichoke is a robust perennial whose large inflorescences are harvested before their bracts (or leaves) have opened.

BORAGE, MARIGOLD, AND NASTURTIUM

Many flowers like borage, marigold, and nasturtium are picked to brighten up salads and vegetable platters with their colorful petals. If you let them go to seed, they will happily self-seed in your garden, making them particularly easy to grow.

→ AVAILABILITY OF MAJOR FLOWER VEGETABLES

Keep in mind that growing seasons vary according to your region. This chart is based on USDA hardiness zones 6–7, but because there can be a great deal of variation even within each zone, check with neighbors or your local agricultural extension office for information specific to your area.

	J	F	M	A	M	J	J	A	S	O	N	D
Artichoke				▓	▓	▓		▓	▓	▓		
Calabrese broccoli							▓	▓	▓	▓	▓	
Cauliflower, summer and fall								▓	▓	▓	▓	

 Harvest

Legumes

Legumes are harvested at various stages of maturity, depending on the variety. For immediate consumption, they are picked once the pod is full and the seeds are fully formed but still tender. For preserving purposes, they should be harvested once the pod has turned yellow because this is a sign it has fully matured. Lentils and chickpeas are harvested at full maturity, whereas green peas are picked while still immature.

Split peas are a pea variety that is rarely grown in gardens, but this is a bit of a shame since they are an excellent vegetable that is easy to store.

Like most legumes, chickpeas are especially rich in carbohydrates and protein.

→ AVAILABILITY OF MAJOR LEGUMES

Keep in mind that growing seasons vary according to your region. This chart is based on USDA hardiness zones 6–7, but because there can be a great deal of variation even within each zone, check with neighbors or your local agricultural extension office for information specific to your area.

	J	F	M	A	M	J	J	A	S	O	N	D
Bush beans												
Chickpeas												
Fava beans												
Lentils												
Peas												
Pole beans												

■ Harvest
■ Storage

A split pea separates into two halves when the outer skin of the pea is removed after harvest.

Root vegetables

The root vegetables group includes bulbs, true roots like turnips and beets, and tubers. Because they are easy to store, many of these vegetables are eaten in winter.

There are several unusual root vegetables that can broaden the range of foods in your garden between November and May. Salsify and scorzonera, for example, are well-known but not often cultivated. Other vegetables are seen even less frequently: Chinese artichokes, mashua, root chervil, skirret, oca, evening primrose, and yacón are all dependable species that are rarely troubled by parasites. The pale-leaf sunflower (*Helianthus strumosus*) is a close relative of the Jerusalem artichoke but has a more delicate flavor. Daikon radishes are large radishes that grow in summer and fall. Yellow nutsedge is an herbaceous perennial plant with rhizome networks that produce small, white, starchy, sugary tubers just before winter. A fall vegetable garden will also happily house other lesser-known root vegetables like burdock, achira, Chinese yam, golden thistle, and rampion.

→ AVAILABILITY OF MAJOR ROOT VEGETABLES

Keep in mind that growing seasons vary according to your region. This chart is based on USDA hardiness zones 6–7, but because there can be a great deal of variation even within each zone, check with neighbors or your local agricultural extension office for information specific to your area.

	J	F	M	A	M	J	J	A	S	O	N	D
Beet, red												
Carrot (depending on variety and planting time)												
Celery root												
Jerusalem artichoke												
Onion												
Parsnip												
Potato (depending on variety and planting time)												
Radish, fall and winter												
Radish, spring												
Radish, summer												
Rutabaga												
Sweet potato												
Turnip, fall												
Turnip, purple top Milan												

Harvest
Storage

Perpetual vegetables

Perpetual vegetables are perennial or shrub vegetables that can be harvested every year and do not need to be uprooted when the growing season ends. Since they can be harvested regularly without having to be replanted, they are often thought of as the absolute best vegetables for spring and fall, and some, like asparagus, rhubarb, and artichokes are—or should be—very common in most spring or fall gardens. Others, like Chinese artichoke, golden thistle, and the perpetual leek are not seen as frequently. A number of less common root vegetables are sold as perpetuals even though they aren't technically true perpetuals. Oca, mashua (pictured above), and the yacón plant do indeed reseed themselves from one year to the next, but they also require shelter from extreme winter cold. You might be saving yourself the cost of the tuber or root system—since you will be sustaining your plantings using plants already in your garden—but those tubers still need to be replanted every year. In short, growing them only because you want to save yourself some work is not the best idea. They take up space in the garden from January to December for a harvest that is sometimes meager, and the amount of weeding—which putting down straw can only reduce in part—is sometimes more of an inconvenience than replanting. It is more reasonable to consider these species as potential additions to more commonly cultivated garden species.

Mushrooms

Mushrooms occupy a special place in the world of living things. Part plant and part animal to some people, something else entirely to others, they are defined by what they lack: they have no roots, stems, leaves, or chlorophyll. The "vegetative" part is the mycelium, a network of overlapping filaments, and on top of this are the reproductive organs, which are the mushrooms themselves. Even though they require special growing techniques, mushrooms can be harvested and used in the kitchen just like vegetables. A botanist might object to my saying this, but to a gardener, vegetables and mushrooms are birds of a feather. Out of the roughly thirty species or varieties of mushrooms that can be grown in the garden, the most cultivated ones are the oyster mushroom, shiitake, and button mushroom.

Herbs

Herbs are edible aromatic plants. Their flavor-enhancing properties make them indispensable companions in the kitchen, and their scent frightens away many garden parasites, thereby limiting the damage they can inflict on your crops. While all of them can be eaten fresh from the garden, preserving them can be a little more complicated. Garlic and chili peppers will keep in cold storage for several months, gherkins will last an entire year in brine or vinegar, and lemon balm, mint, oregano, lavender, stevia, lemon verbena, sage, rosemary, thyme, and bay leaf can be dried in summer and stored for later use. If you harvest dill and coriander seeds when they are ripe and store them somewhere dry, you'll be able to use them for several years.

Like vegetables, herbs can grow as shrubs or annual, biennial, and perennial plants. Perennial and shrub herbs also happen to be perpetual plants.

HERBS FOR TEA

Whether they are fresh or dried and kept in small paper bags, the leaves and shoots from lemon balm, mint, hyssop, rosemary, lemon verbena, stevia, sage, and thyme as well as the buds from lavender, marigold, and various chamomile plants—feverfew (*Tanacetum parthenium*), German chamomile (*Matricaria recutita*), or Roman chamomile (*Chamaemelum nobile*)—can be used to make hot or cold teas and drinks all year long.

→ AVAILABILITY OF MAJOR HERBS

Keep in mind that growing seasons vary according to your region. This chart is based on USDA hardiness zones 6–7, but because there can be a great deal of variation even within each zone, check with neighbors or your local agricultural extension office for information specific to your area.

	J	F	M	A	M	J	J	A	S	O	N	D
Basil						▓	▓	▓	▓			
Bay leaf	░	░	░	░	░	▓	▓	▓	▓	░	░	░
Chervil	░	░		▓	▓			▓	▓		░	░
Chili pepper	░	░	░	░	░	▓	▓	▓	▓	░	░	░
Chives		░	░	▓	▓	▓	▓	▓	▓	▓	░	
Cilantro (leaves) (see footnote 1)						▓	▓	▓	▓			
Coriander (seeds)	░	░	░	░	░			▓	▓	░	░	░
Dill (leaves) [1]					▓	▓	▓	▓				
Dill (seeds)	░	░	░	░	░			▓	▓	░	░	░
Garlic [2]	░	░	░			▓	▓	▓	░	░	░	░
Gherkin	░	░	░	░	░	▓	▓	▓	▓	░	░	░
Lavender	░	░	░	░	░	▓	▓	▓	░	░	░	░
Lemon balm	░	░	░	░	▓	▓	▓	▓	▓	▓	░	░
Lemon verbena	░	░	░	░	▓	▓	▓	▓	▓	░	░	░
Lovage				▓	▓	▓	▓	▓	▓			
Mint	░	░	░	▓	▓	▓	▓	▓	▓	▓	░	░
Oregano	░	░	░	▓	▓	▓	▓	▓	▓	▓	░	░
Parsley, flat-leaf and curly-leaf [3]		░	▓	▓	▓	▓	▓	▓	▓	▓	░	░
Rosemary		░	▓	▓	▓	▓	▓	▓	▓	▓	░	░
Sage		░	▓	▓	▓	▓	▓	▓	▓	▓	░	░
Shallot							▓	░	░	░		
Spring onion				▓	▓	▓	▓	▓	▓			
Stevia	░					▓	▓	▓	▓			░
Tarragon				▓	▓	▓	▓	▓	▓			
Thyme	░	░	░	▓	▓	▓	▓	▓	▓	▓	░	░

▓ Harvest
░ Storage or preservation

(1) In order to have a steady supply all summer, dill and cilantro require three to five sowings between April and August.
(2) Garlic preservation potential varies depending on the variety: purple garlic has a lower storage capability than white garlic, which in turn does not stay fresh as long as pink garlic does.
(3) A continuous fresh harvest requires three annual sowings: the first in March, the second in June, and the third in late August.

There are many more uncommon herbs that are perfectly at home in a fall garden. Depending on the hardiness zone where you live, you might try garden cress, ramsons, angelica, horseradish, annual and perennial savory, cumin, hyssop, creeping thyme, or marjoram. A number of other species like Mexican tarragon, giant hyssop, Moldavian dragonhead, saffron crocus, tansy, society garlic, sweet violet, and scarlet beebalm are ornamental herbs that look as lovely as they taste. Among my favorite herbs are Chinese chives, which have a curious garlic scent and are grown like common chives; Welsh onions, which look like shallots and grow like them too; Vietnamese coriander, which is easier to grow than cilantro even though it isn't as hardy; lemon grass; and tree onion.

But the list of herbs you can grow doesn't stop there, and any of the following are wonderful to have in your own backyard: wormwood, sand leek, anise, woodruff, southernwood, costmary, lesser calamint, caraway, sweet cicely, scurvy grass, paracress, fennel, marshmallow, sweet grass, curry plant, hairy mountain mint, perilla, parsley root, salad burnet, rue, pineapple sage, Andean silver-leaf sage, clary sage, bog sage, valerian.

While the flavor of parsley root leaves is similar to common parsley, the root itself tastes more like parsnip, carrot, celery root, or hazelnut

Best in small doses . . .

Don't go overboard with rare vegetables and herbs, especially if you are just getting your garden started. They are not always easy to grow and can be difficult to master. They also require time and consistent attention. If you do want to give it a try, do a test run before growing a lot of them in your garden.

The jostaberry is a fruitful and very hardy bush whose sour berries are wonderful in juices, jellies, and jams.

Fruits and nuts

Fruits are a little like vegetables, but sweeter. In fact, the distinction is not always easy to make—after all, isn't it just as pleasant to bite into a cherry tomato from the garden as it is a raspberry or a blackberry? Rhubarb is a particularly difficult species to classify: is it a vegetable, herb, or fruit? For our purposes, it is the edible end result that makes a crop a vegetable or a fruit (rhubarb is a fruit because it is generally consumed in pies or compotes). Unlike vegetables, most of which need to be replanted every year, fruit trees and bushes are perennial plants that will remain in your garden anywhere from five to one hundred years or even longer, depending on the species.

Most fruits are consumed or prepared for eating immediately after being harvested. Many like strawberries, raspberries, apricots, peaches, and figs don't keep for very long. Early harvest apple and pear varieties can be consumed a few days after harvesting and will keep for a few weeks. Storage varieties are preserved in a root cellar and can be eaten for most of the winter.

There are several more unusual fruit trees and bushes that make nice additions to the varieties that are often seen in the garden. Black currant and jostaberry (a black currant-gooseberry hybrid) are not so much berries to be eaten in summer as they are fruits to be turned into jelly, jam, and various drinks. They are easy to introduce into a garden and will grow just like red currants. Wild strawberries

→ AVAILABILITY OF MAJOR FRUITS AND NUTS

Keep in mind that growing seasons vary according to your region. This chart is based on USDA hardiness zones 6–7, but because there can be a great deal of variation even within each zone, check with neighbors or your local agricultural extension office for information specific to your area.

	J	F	M	A	M	J	J	A	S	O	N	D
Almond	▨	▨						▓	▨	▨	▨	▨
Apple (depending on variety)	▨	▨	▨					▓	▨	▨	▨	▨
Apricot (depending on variety)							▓	▓				
Blackberry								▓				
Cherry (depending on variety)				▓								
Fig (depending on variety)							▓					
Gooseberry						▓						
Grape (depending on variety)									▓			
Hazelnut			▨						▓	▨	▨	▨
Kiwi	▨	▨	▨								▓	▨
Peach (depending on variety)							▓					
Pear (depending on variety)	▨	▨						▓			▨	▨
Plum (depending on variety)								▓				
Quince										▓		
Raspberry (depending on variety)							▓	▓				
Red currant (depending on variety)					▓							
Rhubarb				▓	▓							
Shadbush						▓						
Strawberry (depending on variety)							▓	▓				

▓ Harvest
▨ Stockage

and musk strawberries are strawberry plants whose small fruits are red or white, depending on the variety. Both varieties make excellent groundcover for a variety of bushes. Loquat and Cornelian cherry (*Cornus mas*) bushes both bear firm, hardy fruits. Blueberries and cranberries are more difficult to introduce into a garden because, like the chestnut tree, they tend to prefer acidic soil. The Japanese nashi pear tree is a fragile plant and can be difficult to grow. Persimmons are relatively cold-resistant—they can survive at temperatures as low as 5°F (-15°C) and even 0°F (-18°C)—and are being planted more and more often in home gardens. Olive and jujube trees are Southern Mediterranean trees that need a similar climate to produce fruits. Walnut trees are not seen as often because of their large size at maturity and the long years required for their nuts to appear. If you have one on your land already, treasure it.

Orchards, fruit forests, and high biodiversity hedges . . .

Traditionally, fruit bushes were always planted along the edges of vegetable gardens and fruit trees were planted separately in orchards. Today we can use the principles of agroforestry—a land-use system for growing trees, fruit bushes, and vegetables together in harmony—to plant them in a variety of different ways. The forest garden uses several perennial plants—chosen either for the food they provide or for their agronomic benefits (the ability to fix nitrogen from the air, for example)—to naturally establish tree cover. A high biodiversity hedge, on the other hand, is a row of many different bush and tree species grown next to each other. In regions with lots of sunlight, in what is called an oasis garden, vegetable plants and bushes are protected under a parasol formed by the branches of tall fruit trees. Whatever the style or model being used, together the various species should make up a cultivated ecosystem that is diversified, stable, and sustainable.

"Kazanlak" is a Cornelian cherry variety whose fruits measure nearly 1.5 inches (4 cm) in length.

Beehives in the orchard

Without bees to pollinate flowers, there would be no fruit! And without flowers for the bees to forage in, there would be no honey! The three elements—flowers, fruit, and honey—are therefore inextricably linked. It is not surprising that so many gardeners are passionate about beekeeping . . . and that quite a lot of beekeepers are passionate about gardening!

The chicken and the egg

The idea of including a chicken coop in a kitchen garden is nothing new: it wasn't so long ago that every rural home had its own chickens. This key part of family food self-sufficiency has, unfortunately, been almost entirely lost, but within the last decade it has seen a significant revival. A sign of the times, perhaps?

Eggs

Adopting a few hens will provide you with fresh eggs every day to accompany your vegetables. You can eat them scrambled, boiled, fried, or in an omelet, and you can also use them to make pies and cakes. Don't worry—you won't need too many chickens! Depending on the time of year and the breed you choose, six hens will give you three to five eggs a day.

Boiling and roasting chicken

Our grandparents' chicken flocks were a source of white meat that cost them almost nothing. Roosters born on the farm that were not destined for breeding, along with any extra young hens, were eaten for their meat once they reached the age of five or six months. Older hens that were laying less and less after two or three years were usually simmered for hours in a stock pot. "Sacrificing" a chicken these days is not for everyone—I personally am incapable of doing it!—but if you have a sturdier heart than I do, your roosters and hens between six months and a year old and your older hens will supply you with plenty of white meat to roast or boil. The flavor, so they say, is outstanding.

A small flock of chickens will provide you with fresh eggs to collect every day.

GRAIN AND STRAW

Chickens are essentially granivores, but they won't turn up their beaks at greens or leftover fish and meat. If the size of your land allows (larger than 1,800 square yards (about ⅓ acre), why not grow your own grain to feed them? You can also use the straw from the harvest as organic matter for mulch or chicken litter.

2
A FERTILE AND GENEROUS SOIL

Vegetables, herbs, fruits, eggs, honey, and grains make up the foundation of food self-sufficiency. But where should we start to make sure we have as much as we need? Well, as the ancient Greek philosopher Xenophanes once said, "All things come from earth, and all things end by becoming earth." He was certainly right: a soft, humus-bearing soil that is sufficiently damp without being too wet is the ideal environment for the vast majority of vegetables, herbs, fruit trees and bushes, grains for humans and animals, and even flowers, which bees need to produce honey.

Plants need the soil...

Plant roots anchor themselves solidly in the ground where they draw in the minerals they need to grow. Aerated soil ensures plenty of air circulation—oxygen is vital to root development—and water is stored in the soil's micropores to be sent to the plants as needed. Even if it does not always provide all of the water that plants need, the soil is nevertheless their primary and most important water reserve.

... and the soil needs plants

Land that is not covered by plants will become poor, and in its natural state, bare ground will not remain empty for very long. Plant root secretions break down mineral matter and soften the soil. By dropping their leaves in the fall, plants provide the soil with organic matter that helps the microflora and microfauna already in the ground. In this way, the aerial and underground portions of wild and cultivated plants are the engine driving microbial dynamics within the soil, whether that soil happens to be cultivated or not.

PLANTS FEED ON MORE THAN JUST SOIL . . .

Plants cannot get everything they need from the soil. Carbon and oxygen, which together make up 88 percent of plant tissues, come from carbon dioxide present in the atmosphere. The major (nitrogen, phosphate, potassium) and minor (magnesium, iron, copper, etc.) mineral elements that plants find in the soil are essential to their growth but are less significant in terms of the quantity required.

Leaves, pieces of bark, pinecones . . . everything comes from the earth and returns to the earth.

Did you say nitrogen?

Nitrogen is an unconventional mineral element because it is not found in source rock but exists in large quantities in the atmosphere, where it is generally not available to plants. In spite of this fact, nitrogen has a decisive influence on plant growth and is responsible for the vigorous development of the plant's foliage. In organic gardening, the addition of organic matter meets most of the plant's nitrogen needs. While organic matter plays other important roles, of course, this example demonstrates how important it can be in a garden that shuns the use of fertilizers.

Organic matter and humus

Organic matter is made up of cellulose and lignin, and when it decomposes, the end product is humus. This essential soil component is the primary provider of plant nitrogen and exists in two forms in the soil. Young humus is formed by the rapid transformation of cellulosic matter; it is very labile, and plants can use it almost immediately. Old or "stable" humus is composed of lignin and cellulose derivatives. It breaks down slowly—less than 2 percent a year—in a persistent and continuous rhythm.

Organic matter—and not necessarily the mineral elements that make it up—is what determines the structure of the soil.

Loose and aerated soil

Just as organic matter improves the mineral richness of the soil, it also has a positive effect on the soil's texture. It limits compactions caused by trampling and precipitation and in so doing improves the soil's looseness and permeability. So, soil that contains plenty of humus is not only rich and fertile; it is also easier to cultivate.

Soil that takes care of itself

Nature functions on its own without a single human around. Plant and animal matter that falls on the ground is crushed and transformed by organisms living in the soil. Part of it is mineralized and reabsorbed by plants, and the rest is transformed into humus. For self-sufficiency and sustainability purposes, you will need to adopt ways of doing things in your garden that mirror the way it would function in nature. Doing this will help you achieve both abundant harvests and a constant improvement of your soil's gardening potential.

Ideally, the cultivated land should wrap around the home.

WHAT ABOUT PARASITES?

Loose and fertile soil, diversified plantings, and pertinent interventions performed at the right time are enough to ensure that your plants will grow well and should limit damage caused by most kinds of pests. Exceptions: carrots, onions, garlic, shallots, and leeks are highly susceptible to vegetable flies and certain fungal diseases, regardless of their growing conditions. In the event of repeated attacks, the best way to limit their impact is to place these vegetables under hoops covered with insect netting.

Flatbed gardening

Generations of gardeners have used flatbed gardening, and, in most cases, it is what works best. There is not as much grueling landscaping work to do because the surface of the ground is maintained and cultivated as it is naturally. A flatbed garden is extremely customizable and gives you plenty of freedom to organize where your plantings will go. If you have good soil, don't think twice about it: this is how you should cultivate it. But even if your soil is of only medium quality, you can improve its growing potential quickly by systematically applying organic matter and mulch. The only soils that require special modifications are: pebbly soils that are extremely heavy and compact due to their clay content, soils that are very light and sandy, and soils that are excessively limey, or, on the contrary, too acidic (pH lower than 5.5).

What if I have very low-quality soil?

It is both time-consuming and costly to transform an entire area of imperfect soil, but berms, sheet mulching, and raised beds can all help you improve the soil in a specific location. Later on, these enriched areas are where you will plant seeds and transplants.

To make them easier to cultivate, your berm, sheet mulching area, or raised bed should generally be no wider than 1.30 yards (1.20 m). It can be a long and often painstaking process to set them up, but once you're finished you can start planting things like tomatoes, cucumbers, zucchini, and squash immediately. These vegetables love soil rich in organic matter and they don't mind if it is only partially decomposed.

A TEST GARDEN

A square foot garden typically consists of a 4 foot x 4 foot (1.2 m x 1.2 m) raised bed divided into a grid of sixteen smaller squares. Crop yields may be low, but because it is so easy to tend and harvest, it is ideal for trying out new species and varieties of vegetables and herbs before they grow to their full size in the vegetable garden.

Berms, sheet mulching, and raised beds

A berm is a roughly 28-inch (70-cm) tall mound of soil high in organic matter. The soil is stacked in layers so the largest and least decomposed pieces of organic matter are on the bottom, and the finest and most decomposed are on the top. This soil mixture is deposited onto a cleared patch of land to form the berm. Sheet mulching also uses layers of organic matter but they are piled on top of a layer of cardboard, generally reaching about 2 feet (60 cm) in height (see photo above). Raised beds are built using wooden planks around 12 inches (30 cm) wide and are filled in with old, more or less decomposed organic matter.

3

WATER INDEPENDENCE AND SOURCING PLANT MATERIAL

The availability of water and plant material will have a significant impact on your harvest, both in terms of quality and quantity. Before planting anything in your garden, make sure you have both of these things available in the volumes you need.

Lettuce is a leaf vegetable that is particularly demanding when it comes to water.

Water availability

Maintaining a garden—especially when this involves caring for young transplants—requires water. Ideally, especially in areas that receive winter snowfall, the soil fills with water in spring, and periodic summer showers keep the land relatively hydrated. However, even a novice gardener knows that sometimes gardens need additional watering. Plants can adapt to fluctuations in water availability to a certain extent but going without it completely would be quite a challenge. During warm weather, if it doesn't rain, each week you will need access to a permanent water supply of about 132 gallons for every cultivated 120 square yards (500 liters per cultivated 100 square meters). It is best to plan for even more to protect yourself from a prolonged summer drought. Remember that many regions have water restriction policies during heat waves, which means you will only have occasional access to municipal water.

Rainwater is naturally soft water that is also untreated, making it the best water for watering.

Collecting rainwater

The advantage of using rainwater—which, incidentally, is excellent for watering plants—is that it is available everywhere. Depending on the year and the region you live in, you should be able to collect between 132 and 264 gallons (500 and 1,000 liters) of water per square yard of roof. The collection system can be attached to your gutter and even a very average handyman will be able to do it. The limiting factor is usually the storage capacity of your tanks, not the amount of potentially retrievable water.

Choosing the right storage tanks

Depending on your needs and the average precipitation in your area, opt for one or more aboveground tanks or one large underground storage tank. Aboveground tanks will not hold more than 264 gallons (1,000 liters) but you can hook them together so that one collection mechanism fills several tanks. Underground tanks are typically made of polyethylene or steel and can store up to 2,640 gallons (10,000 liters) of water.

Pumped water

The presence of a water table close to the surface means you can pump as much water for your garden as you need. If the water table is less than 6.5 or 7.5 yards (6 or 7 meters) from the surface, all you need is a galvanized pipe fitted with a water well drill bit. This pipe can be raised up on one or several risers and then you can install a manual, thermal, or electric pump on top. If the water table is deeper than that, you—or someone else—will have to install a submersible pump.

WATER WISELY

Always make watering young seedlings and newly planted cultivars your top priority. As they grow, vegetables and fruit trees will regulate their water needs. It is generally a better idea to water abundantly but less frequently as opposed to watering in small quantities at short intervals. Water in the morning in spring and fall, and in the evening in the heart of summer. And remember: neophyte gardeners—and sometimes even those with a great deal of experience—often have a tendency to water too much instead of not enough.

Meeting your own organic matter needs

The soil is colonized by countless microorganisms that break down mineral and organic matter giving plants access to certain elements they need to grow. There is a reason people used to use large quantities of manure to increase soil fertility and crop yields: the soil's physicochemical dynamics are directly correlated with the presence of sufficient quantities of organic matter.

Organic matter from your own home . . .

You can use all kinds of recycled organic matter from home in your garden—a complete list of examples would be too long! While kitchen waste should be kept for your poultry (unless it's fully composted), you can add: chicken manure; straw from harvested grain; grass clippings; wilted annual, biennial, or perennial plants; soil blocks that have finished their season; repotting soils; old compost; and dead fall leaves to the garden just as they are. Chopped wood and other woody residue, however, should be chipped beforehand. Whatever you decide to use, one thing is certain: what comes from the garden must return to the garden!

It should be said that not all organic matter is created equal. Some is rich in cellulose and lignin; other kinds contain higher quantities of nitrogen. Because it balances the nitrogen from the animal excrement with the cellulose and lignin contained in straw and litter, manure makes the ideal organic amendment, but there are plenty of other good options: the nitrogen/carbon return is also very satisfactory in young branches from fruit trees and bushes, as well as in green manure that is dug in or mowed once the plants' flowers have bloomed.

. . . and organic matter from other sources

Don't overlook opportunities to source organic matter from other people. If you live in a small town or rural area, it is not unusual for farmers and horse breeders to have old straw and manure that they don't need. Making a few telephone calls to neighbors or seizing an opportunity online could potentially provide you with large volumes of organic matter, which is particularly helpful if you are starting a garden from scratch.

WOOD CHIPS

Wood chips from fruit-bearing trees and bushes take a long time to decompose—often longer than eighteen months—and are not ideal for the vegetable garden. But if you spread some around the base of those same woody plants, wood chips will boost microbial activity in the soil (nitrogen-fixing bacteria in particular). This will help you save water and limit weed growth for months!

Grass spread in a shallow layer around newly planted vegetables breaks down quickly.

Green manure

If you find yourself wishing you had more organic matter, consider planting green manure. These plants can be grown on a parcel that is unused, waiting to be cultivated, or even after harvest. Phacelia and buckwheat are planted in late spring and are mowed after blooming. Yellow mustard, rapeseed, and turnip rape, which germinate at 43°F to 46°F (6°C to 8°C), can be planted early in the spring or in late fall. Some green manure crops like alfalfa and clover can be left in the same area for two or three years and offer multiple harvests each year.

WEEDS AS GREEN MANURE?

Garden weeds like chickweed, three-seeded mercury, and groundsel can improve soil fertility like any other green manure if they are pulled up and added to the soil before they go to seed. They also prevent nitrogen from being washed out of the soil after excessive watering or strong rains in the fall and spring.

Using organic matter in the garden

An easy and effective way to use organic matter is to apply it directly on top of the soil as a mulch. Do this in the fall after the last summer vegetable harvests (tomatoes, eggplants, peppers, cucumbers, etc.) or in May or June after the last spring plantings. You can also spread some around the base of newly planted vegetables and herbs to suppress weeds and limit water evaporation to keep the soil moist. When it's time to enrich the soil again in the fall, the organic matter you put down in early summer will be almost completely decomposed.

4
MAKING YOUR OWN GARDEN SOIL

Garden soil is a must-have for planting seeds and repotting young transplants. Garden stores sell bags in various sizes that are often high quality but also expensive. Not to mention the catastrophic carbon footprint left by their manufacturing process and transportation to their retail location—all the more reason to make your own!

A composite growing medium

Industrial garden soils are made from a variety of materials: brown and blond peat—now often replaced by coconut fibers—compost, sand, and sometimes topsoil. Crushed clay, perlite, pozzolana, and vermiculite are also occasionally mixed in. Actually, it can be very difficult to know exactly what they contain because their labels focus more on the primary ingredients and less on technical information like resistivity or conductivity.

Where to start

The best garden soil is fine and fibrous with good water retention and aeration. To achieve the right structure in your homemade garden soil, you will need to mix topsoil from your garden with a large volume of green compost and composted chicken manure. If your soil is high in clay, or if your compost is old and very compacted, adding coarse sand will loosen the soil and promote drainage (fine sand will not improve the quality of your garden soil). To get started, first gather everything you need to make your compost.

Woody residues will decompose more quickly if they are chipped before being composted.

Making green compost

You can make green compost using leftover plant material from garden maintenance, or you can grow green manure crops specifically for this purpose. Any organic matter from your garden will work, but larger pieces like cabbage cores should be cut with shears into small pieces or chipped. The same goes for wood cuttings.

For every 220 pounds (100 kg) of plant matter, you will only end up with between 65 and 75 pounds (30 and 35 kg) of compost, so plan to start with a large amount. It will take between six months and one year to have enough old and sufficiently decomposed compost to make your garden soil. Start composting in early spring because to develop well, compost needs the strong heat of summer.

From plant material to compost

1 Start your compost pile in the shade, if you can, on a patch of ground that has been aerated with a spading fork or broadfork.

2. Once you have all of the organic compost materials you need, add them in layers to form a dense, compact pile. If you are composting a wide variety of items—old and recent grass clippings, dry grass, old hay, manure, straw, dead leaves, wood cuttings, wilted plants, vegetable waste, etc.—mix them together as thoroughly as you can.

3. Water immediately and thoroughly.

4. The pile will quickly heat up and can reach temperatures as high as 176°F (80°C). When this happens, use a pitchfork to turn it.

5. Water again, but this time do not soak the pile. By late fall, you will have turned and stirred the pile two or three more times. After sifting your compost through a 12 mm garden sieve, your compost will be ready in January or February.

Good compost is moist but never soaking wet.

Vermicompost

Vermicompost is a special compost that owes its rapid decomposition to various species of earthworms, usually *Eisenia fetida*, the manure worm. It is made in a special composting bin that features one or more decomposition crates. These can be purchased or made by hand, and they will give you excellent results. The only problem is that you will never have enough compost to make large volumes of garden soil!

Composting chicken manure

The litter of straw deposited at the end of the summer in the chicken run is collected in the spring, placed in a pile, and then watered as needed. Because of its rich nutrient content, it will provide a stable base for even the most demanding plants. This pile will also need to be turned two or three times during the summer if you want to be able to use it at the beginning of the following year. During rainy winters, cover the pile with a tarp to keep it from absorbing too much water. Just like green compost, composted manure usually needs to be sifted just before it is added to your garden soil.

If your topsoil has too many large clumps, it needs to be sifted before being used.

Collecting topsoil

Topsoil can be collected from different spots all over the garden. You may even have a pile left over from landscaping. Wherever you take it from, collect the amount you need just before making your garden soil. Don't worry about depriving your garden—the soil you are removing will be returned in the form of garden soil for plantings and transplants. Remove any large clumps and, ideally, sift it through a 7 mm garden sieve.

Mixing your garden soil

Gather the green compost, composted manure, and topsoil into three piles on a small patch of packed earth or a tiled area. Using an electric or thermal concrete mixer is the easiest way to mix your soil. Just shovel the materials into the mixer in the following proportions: seven shovelfuls of compost, three of dampened topsoil from the garden, and one shovelful of composted chicken manure. If the mixture seems too compact to

Once collected and composted, straw litter from the chicken run will become part of the garden soil.

Mix the compost, composted manure, and topsoil until thoroughly combined to obtain a loose and aerated substrate.

you, add a shovelful of sand (builder's sand works well).

While the materials for your garden soil can be prepared ahead of time, it is best to use up garden soil within a month after mixing it. If you can, make small batches of your soil blend only when you need it. If this is not possible, you can divide a larger batch into sealed opaque polyethylene bags and keep them for a few extra weeks in a cool, dry place.

DO I HAVE TO USE DIFFERENT KINDS OF SOIL FOR SEEDS, CUTTINGS, AND REPOTTED PLANTS?

Garden centers sell specific soils for every situation. While certain garden species like rhododendrons, orchids, and cacti do indeed require special soil, in my experience this is not the case in the kitchen garden. If the soil you used to repot your plants seems too clumpy for your seeds or cuttings, just sift it through a 4 mm garden sieve.

5 SEED PRODUCTION

The fact that a tiny seed removed one year ago from the pulp of a ripe tomato can, in just a few months, produce a new plant that is 6.5 feet (2 meters) tall and bearing its own fruit is the epitome of gardening magic. This is why it's so tempting—especially in a garden designed to be self-sufficient—to repeat this process with every plant species and variety: plant the seed, bring the plant to maturity, and save the seed to plant again next year.

Simple, but also complicated...

The difficult parts of producing your own seeds have more to do with the complexity and diversity of the plant world than the actual method, which is relatively straightforward. The longevity of garden plants, their botanical classification—annual, biennial, perennial—their hardiness, flowering and seed maturation periods, fertilization methods, and seed viability vary tremendously depending on the species, so much so that it would be unrealistic to propose only one way of collecting seeds from all the plants in your garden. Every species is in fact a special case.

Seeds come in all different shapes, colors, and sizes—no two look exactly alike!

45

Annuals, biennials, and perennials

Annual crops germinate, bloom, produce seeds, and die within a single year. Biennials germinate and form a rosette of leaves the first year before blooming, producing seeds, and dying the second year. To make things even more complicated, some hardy annuals sown in the second half of summer behave like biennials, and vice versa: many biennials planted in the spring will produce seeds the same year they are planted! Perennials remain in the ground for several years; they bloom and spread their seeds every year. Since it is not necessary to replant perennials every year, collecting their seeds may be less of a priority than saving annual and biennial seeds. In fact, a number of perennials like lemon balm, hyssop, and rosemary can easily be propagated by cuttings instead of seeds.

Male, female, and hermaphroditic flowers

Some plants have both male and female flowers on the same plant (monoecious) while others separate their male and female flowers onto separate plants (dioecious). Hermaphroditic plants house the male and female parts within the same flower. How the sexual parts of the plant are separated (or not) is important information to know when saving seeds because it determines how the seeds are produced.

Cross-pollinating and self-pollinating plants

Female flowers on cross-pollinating (or "allogamous") plants have to be fertilized with pollen from another plant of the same species, either by the wind or with the help of pollinating insects. Self-pollinating (or "autogamous") plants carry hermaphroditic flowers whose ovules are fertilized by the male pollen that is present with them in the same bloom. In the case of the tomato—a self-pollinating plant—fertilization generally takes place inside the flower bud before it even blooms.

Seed longevity

If they are stored somewhere dry and cool, seeds can sustain their germination power for several years. Seeds from the Brassicaceae family (cabbage, radish, turnip, etc.) can be saved for a long time, often eight years or more. Cucurbitaceae (squash, melon, cucumber, etc.), Solanaceae (tomato, pepper, and chili pepper), and Asteraceae (lettuce and chicory) seeds last around five years. Seeds from Alliums (onion, spring onion, chives, etc.), Apiaceae (celery, carrot, parsley, etc.), and Fabaceae (peas, beans, etc.) usually do not last longer than three years.

To avoid confusion, label your seed containers with the species, variety, and the date you harvested them.

NO NEED TO DO IT EVERY YEAR . . .

It is not necessary to collect seeds each year from every vegetable and herb you'd like to grow again. Depending on their shelf life, you may only need to collect seeds every two to eight years. Plant and seed swaps at garden centers are great opportunities to trade your surplus seed with other gardeners (as long as you're sure they are reliable!).

The tables on pages 48 and 49 indicate the shelf life for seeds from major vegetable crops. Of course, all gardeners have seen tomato seeds that germinated after more than six years and radish or basil seeds that did the same after ten years or more, so these are merely guidelines. Simply put, if you keep your seeds for longer than the length of time indicated, it is a good idea to test the quality of your stored seeds with a germination test.

→ SEED VIABILITY—VEGETABLES

Seed type	Longevity under proper storage conditions
Artichoke	6 years
Arugula	5 years
Asparagus	5 years
Beans, all	3 years
Cabbages, all (including Asian cabbages)	5 years
Calabrese broccoli	5 years
Carrot	3 years
Celery	6 years
Celery root	6 years
Chickpea	3 years
Chicories, all (including endive)	5 years
Cucumber	8 years
Dandelion	3 years
Eggplant	2 years
Fennel	3 years
Leek	2 years
Lentil	3 years
Lettuce, all	3 years
Mâche	4 years
Melon and watermelon	5 years
Miner's lettuce	4 years
Onion	2 years
Parsnip	Less than 1 year
Peas	2 years
Pepper	4 years
Physalis peruviana	8 years
Purslane	6 years
Radishes, all	6 years
Rutabaga	4 years
Sorrel	2 years
Spinach	4 years
Squash, all (including zucchini)	5 years
Sweet corn	2 years
Swiss chard, beet	6 years
Tomato	4 years
Turnips, all	4 years

→ SEED VIABILITY—HERBS

Seed type	Longevity under proper storage conditions
Basil	8 years
Bay leaf	2 months
Chili pepper	4 years
Chives	2 years
Cilantro/Coriander	5 years
Dill	2 years
Gherkin	8 years
Lemon balm	3 years
Lovage	2 years
Oregano	1 year
Parsley, curly-leaf	2 years
Parsley, flat-leaf	2 years
Rhubarb	3 years
Rosemary	1 year
Sage	3 years
Spring onion	2 years
Thyme	3 years

Only store seeds in paper bags once they are completely dry.

Testing your seeds

Testing seed viability is not very complicated but does require a little bit of organization. On the plus side, it will save you useless work and the terrible inconvenience of sowing seeds that have lost all or part of their germinative potential. This test only needs to be carried out on seeds that have passed the longevity date or that appear to have a problem: mold, discoloring, shriveled appearance, etc.

How to test your seeds

1. Place a piece of absorbent paper (blotting paper or paper towel) in a saucer. Write the variety of seed you are testing on the paper.

2. If the seeds are small, place twenty-five seeds on the piece of paper. For peas and beans, place ten seeds on each paper.

3. Spray the paper and seeds with water before covering them with a slightly raised glass or plexiglass plate to keep them from drying out. This transparent cover will make it easier to keep track of how damp the seeds are (they shouldn't be soaking wet, but it is important that the paper and seeds never dry out during the test).

4. Leave the seeds somewhere that gets plenty of light with a temperature between 72°F and 77°F (22°C and 25°C).

5. Check for germination five days after placing the seeds on the absorbent paper.

6. Record the appearance of radicles and young shoots every two days. Do this three times.

7. Count the number of small seeds that have germinated and multiply it by four (or by ten for large seeds). This will give you each variety's germination percentage.

8. Depending on how each type of seed is planted—via broadcast seeding or with a precision seeder—the germination percentage should be somewhere between 60 and 100 percent.

9. Eliminate any groups of seeds that do not meet the above criteria.

January is the best month for testing your old seeds.

CAN I TRUST THE EXPIRATION DATES ON STORE-BOUGHT SEED PACKETS?

This is a question that all gardeners have asked themselves at some point and the answer is clear: no, the dates on seed packets are not reliable. They often extend far beyond the longevity recommendations listed in the previous pages' tables, and what's more, there is no guarantee that the seeds in the packet come from the most recent harvest. It would be more honest of professional seed dealers to label each packet with the year the seeds were harvested.

Isolation cages

You won't find isolation cages in a store; you will have to make them yourself! This rectangular structure can be made out of wood or metal and should measure at least 2 feet (60 cm) on each side. Once covered with insect netting, it can be placed over your plants before the first blooms appear and remain in place until the first fruits arrive. You can then remove it and the self-fertilized fruits will continue ripening until the seeds are ready to be harvested.

Precautions to take

Depending on the plant, collecting seeds is either easy, moderately difficult, quite complicated, or, in certain cases, impossible (French tarragon, for example, does not produce seeds, and seeds from the stevia and lemon verbena plants may not mature in cold climates). While the majority of plants produce seeds, in order to maintain genetic purity and varietal characteristics you will need to take certain precautions with some plants to avoid unwanted cross-pollination. The easiest approach is to cultivate only one variety of the plant in question or only let one variety go to seed. Unfortunately, this is not always possible, and in this case, you will need to isolate seed-producing plants in cages. By preventing pollinating insects from intruding, the cage removes any risk of accidental cross-pollination.

The particularities of biennial plants

Biennial plants only bloom the second year, which makes removing their seeds more complicated, especially for crops like onions, beets, and Nantes carrots that are less hardy in certain climates (winter carrot varieties can be left in the ground under straw). These seed-producers will have to spend the winter sheltered from the cold as bulbs or roots before being replanted the following spring.

Harvesting chili seeds does not require any special precautions.

Once they have been removed from the pulp, pumpkin seeds will need to be dried before storage.

Hand pollinating cucurbits

Plants in the squash family—pumpkin, red kuri squash, butternut and other winter squash, zucchini and pattypan squash, melons, cucumbers, and gherkins—are all monoecious, meaning their male and female flower parts are on the same plant. Varieties in this family are also highly allogamous and will easily hybridize with one another. If you want to preserve the integrity of the varieties in your garden, you can hand pollinate these plants thanks to their large blooms and many seeds. To do this, the night before the blooms open, isolate the male flowers from the female flowers in insect netting bags 12 inches (30 centimeters) long. The next day, once the blooms have opened, take off the bags and use a paintbrush to remove some pollen from the stamen of a male flower and rub it on the stigma of a female flower of the same variety. Cover the female flower again and keep it in the protective bag until a young fruit appears. Remove the bag and mark the fertilized fruits with a piece of twine. Once the fruits are ripe, you can retrieve and dry the seeds before storing them somewhere cool and protected from moisture.

→ MAJOR VEGETABLE SEEDS TO SAVE

Seed type	Flower and pollination type	Level of difficulty	Precautions
Artichoke	Perennial—Hermaphroditic—Cross-pollinating	Medium	Only cultivate one variety. Hybridizes with cardoon. Spring propagation by offshoots is possible and even preferable.
Arugula, cultivated and wild	Annual or biennial—Hermaphroditic—Cross-pollinating	Easy	Harvest seeds at full maturity. Cultivated and wild arugula will not cross with each other (wild varieties belong to the genus Diplotaxis).
Asparagus	Perennial—Dioecious	Difficult	Only cultivate one variety. Select and tag male and female plants the year before you collect seeds. In the spring, do not harvest spears from the male and female plants you choose for saving seeds.
Bean, bush and pole	Annual—Hermaphroditic—Usually self-pollinating	Easy	Avoid cultivating two varieties side by side if you want to harvest seeds from them. Only harvest seeds from early plantings that have fully developed.
Bean, fava	Annual—Hermaphroditic—Cross-pollinating	Easy	Only cultivate one variety. Only remove seeds from fully ripened pods.
Beet, red	Biennial—Hermaphroditic—Cross-pollinating	Difficult	Only let one variety go to seed. Protect the mother plant from frost in winter and replant it in the spring. Hybridizes with Swiss chard. If necessary, place plants under an isolation cage.
Brussels sprouts	Biennial—Hermaphroditic—Cross-pollinating	Medium	Do not harvest Brussels sprouts from the seed-producing plant. Leave it in the ground all winter. Hybridizes with turnip, radish, and other members of the cabbage family. Only let one variety go to seed. If necessary, place plants under an isolation cage.
Cabbage, Asian, including bok choy and Napa cabbage	Biennial—Hermaphroditic—Cross-pollinating	Medium	Do not save seeds from the plants that go to seed in the first year. Winter the seed-producing plants under a movable tunnel. Hybridizes with turnip, radish, and other members of the cabbage family. Only let one variety go to seed. If necessary, place under an isolation cage.

Seed type	Flower and pollination type	Level of difficulty	Precautions
Cabbage, green and red	Biennial— Hermaphroditic— Cross-pollinating	Difficult	Winter the seed-producing plant under a movable tunnel. Hybridizes with turnip, radish, and other members of the cabbage family. Only let one variety go to seed. If necessary, place under an isolation cage.
Calabrese broccoli	Biennial— Hermaphroditic— Cross-pollinating	Difficult	Protect seed-producing plants from frost. Hybridizes with turnip, radish, and other cabbage family members. Only let one variety go to seed. If necessary, place plants under an isolation cage.
Carrot	Biennial— Hermaphroditic— Cross-pollinating	Medium	Leave the roots in the ground and cover with a thick layer of straw to protect them from cold. Less hardy varieties can be kept in sand in a cellar and planted in the garden in March. Only let one variety go to seed each year.
Cauliflower, summer and fall	Biennial— Hermaphroditic— Cross-pollinating	Difficult	Protect the plant from cold temperatures in winter. Hybridizes with turnip, radish, and other cabbage family members. Only let one variety go to seed. If necessary, place under an isolation cage.
Celery	Biennial— Hermaphroditic— Cross-pollinating	Medium	Protect seed-producing plants from frost. Hybridizes with celery root. Only let one variety go to seed. If necessary, place plants under an isolation cage.
Celery root	Biennial— Hermaphroditic— Cross-pollinating	Medium	Winter the roots in sand in a cellar and replant them in the spring. Hybridizes with celery. Only let one variety go to seed. If necessary, place plants under an isolation cage.
Chickpea	Annual— Hermaphroditic— Generally self-pollinating	Easy	Set aside some of the seeds harvested for eating to use for planting.

Seed type	Flower and pollination type	Level of difficulty	Precautions
Cucumber	Annual—Monoecious—Cross-pollinating	Medium	Hybridizes with gherkins but not with squash, zucchini, or melon. Only cultivate one variety. Alternatively, use hand pollination or an isolation cage.
Dandelion	Perennial—Reproduces asexually through apomixis*	Easy	Harvest seeds at maturity.
Eggplant	Annual—Hermaphroditic—Cross-pollinating—Occasionally self-fertilizes	Medium	Only cultivate one variety or place the seed-producing plant in an isolation cage.
Endive	Biennial—Hermaphroditic—Cross-pollinating	Medium	Do not harvest seeds from plants that go to seed the first year. Leave at least a dozen endive roots in the ground during the winter and protect them with straw. Only let one variety go to seed or use an isolation cage.
Escarole and frisée, summer and fall	Biennial—Hermaphroditic—Cross-pollinating	Medium	Do not take seeds from plants that go to seed the first year. Winter the mother plants under a movable tunnel. Hybridizes with other chicories. Only let one variety go to seed each year. If necessary, place plants under an isolation cage.
Fennel	Annual—Hermaphroditic—Cross-pollinating	Easy	Only cultivate one variety. Hybridizes easily with cultivated or wild perennial fennel. Use an isolation cage as needed.
Kale, curly and red Russian	Biennial—Hermaphroditic—Cross-pollinating	Easy	Leave the seed-producing plant in the ground in winter. Hybridizes with turnip, radish, and other cabbage family members. Only let one variety go to seed. If necessary, place plants under an isolation cage.

(*) Apomixis is a mode of asexual reproduction in which seeds are produced without fertilization, which means there is no risk of hybridization.

Seed type	Flower and pollination type	Level of difficulty	Precautions
Kohlrabi	Biennial—Hermaphroditic—Cross-pollinating	Difficult	Protect the seed-producing plant from winter frost. Hybridizes with turnip, radish, and other cabbage family members. Only let one variety go to seed. If necessary, place under an isolation cage.
Leek	Biennial—Hermaphroditic—Cross-pollinating	Easy	Leave seed-producing plants in the ground for the winter. Does not hybridize with onion or chives. Only let one variety go to seed or use an isolation cage.
Lentils	Annual—Hermaphroditic—Generally self-pollinating	Easy	Set aside some of the seeds you harvest for kitchen use and use them for planting.
Lettuce, all	Annual—Hermaphroditic—Self-pollinating	Easy	Harvest seeds from vigorous plants that were transplanted in early spring and went to seed before the hottest part of summer.
Mâche	Biennial—Hermaphroditic—Cross-pollinating	Easy	Only let one variety go to seed in the spring.
Melon and watermelon	Annual—Monoecious—Cross-pollinating	Easy	Melon and watermelon will not cross with each other or with cucumbers. Only cultivate one variety of each or use hand pollination.
Miner's lettuce	Annual or biennial—Hermaphroditic—Self-pollinating	Easy	Protect the seed-producing plants from cold winter temperatures. Harvest the seeds before full maturity to keep the seedpod from dropping prematurely. Will self-seed.
Onion	Biennial—Hermaphroditic—Cross-pollinating	Difficult	Save seed-producing bulbs in a cool, dry place during the winter and replant them in the spring. Only let one variety go to seed or use isolation cages.
Parsnip	Biennial—Hermaphroditic—Cross-pollinating	Easy	Only cultivate one variety. Overwinter parsnips in the ground. Seeds should be harvested every year because of their short lifespan.
Peas	Annual—Hermaphroditic—Cross-pollinating	Easy	Peas intended for eating should be harvested before maturity, but those you would like to plant should be harvested at full maturity.

Seed type	Flower and pollination type	Level of difficulty	Precautions
Pepper	Annual—Hermaphroditic—Primarily self-pollinating	Easy	Harvest mature seeds from the first fruits that appear. The risk of interhybridization is negligible in a kitchen garden.
Physalis peruviana	Annual—Hermaphroditic—Self-pollinating	Easy	Harvest seeds from fully ripened fruit.
Purslane	Annual—Hermaphroditic—Self-pollinating	Easy	Harvest seeds just before maturity because they have a tendency to fall off once they are ripe. Will self-seed.
Radicchio and wild chicory	Biennial—Hermaphroditic—Cross-pollinating	Medium	Do not take seeds from plants that go to seed the first year. Leave seed-producing plants in the ground during the winter (less hardy varieties will need to be protected from the cold). Hybridizes with other chicories. Only let one variety go to seed each year. If necessary, place plants under an isolation cage.
Radishes, all	Annual or biennial—Hermaphroditic—Cross-pollinating	Medium	Leave seed-producing plants in the ground after harvesting the small spring and summer radishes. Fall radishes can spend the winter in a cellar and be replanted in spring. Only let one variety go to seed or use an isolation cage. Radish varieties cross easily with each other and will also hybridize with cabbage, turnip, and all other Brassicaceae.
Rutabaga	Biennial—Hermaphroditic—Cross-pollinating	Easy	Only let one variety go to seed. Rutabaga will not cross with turnip.
Savoy cabbage	Biennial—Hermaphroditic—Cross-pollinating	Medium	Leave the seed-producing plant in the ground for the winter. Hybridizes with turnip, radish, and other cabbage family members. Only let one variety go to seed. If necessary, place under an isolation cage.
Sorrel	Perennial—Dioecious—Cross-pollinating	Easy	Only let male and female plants of the same variety go to seed. Alternatively, use an isolation cage. Harvesting seeds is not necessary for self-seeding varieties.

Seed type	Flower and pollination type	Level of difficulty	Precautions
Spinach	Biennial—Dioecious—Cross-pollinating	Medium	Do not remove leaves from seed-producing plants in winter. In the spring, let the male and female plants go to flower (or bolt). Only cultivate one variety.
Squash, various, including butternut squash, turban squash, red kuri squash, and pumpkin	Annual—Monoecious—Cross-pollinating	Medium	All squash hybridize with each other. Use hand pollination or an isolation cage.
Sweet corn	Annual—Monoecious—Cross-pollinating	Easy	Only cultivate one variety.
Swiss chard	Biennial—Hermaphroditic—Cross-pollinating	Medium	Only let one variety go to seed. Leave the seed-producing plants in the ground for the winter and protect them from the cold. Warning: Swiss chard hybridizes with beets.
Tomato	Annual—Hermaphroditic—Primarily self-pollinating	Easy	Harvest seeds from the best-looking fruits of each variety once they are fully ripened. The risk of interhybridization is negligible in a kitchen garden.
Turnips, all	Biennial—Hermaphroditic—Cross-pollinating	Medium	Only let one variety go to seed. Winter the mother plants indoors and replant them in the spring. Hybridizes with radishes and other cabbage family members. If necessary, place plant under an isolation cage.
Zucchini and pattypan squash	Annual—Monoecious—Cross-pollinating	Medium	Hybridizes with other squash. Use hand pollination or an isolation cage.

Tomato seeds are some of the easiest to harvest. →

→ MAJOR HERB SEEDS TO SAVE

Seed type	Flower and pollination type	Level of difficulty	Precautions
Basil	Annual– Hermaphroditic– Cross-pollinating	Medium	All basils will cross with each other. Only cultivate one variety or use an isolation cage.
Bay leaf	Dioecious shrub– Cross-pollinating	Difficult	You should see berries appear if you plant one male plant and one female plant. Sow the seeds as soon as you have harvested them because they will only be viable for two months.
Chili pepper	Annual– Hermaphroditic– Generally self-pollinating	Easy	Harvest seeds when the fruit is completely ripe. The risk of interhybridization is negligible in a kitchen garden. In the event of accidental hybridization between a sweet and hot pepper, the genes of the hot pepper usually win out.
Chives	Perennial– Hermaphroditic– Cross-pollinating	Medium	Only let one variety go to seed. Some recent varieties do not bloom and can only be propagated by division.
Cilantro	Annual– Hermaphroditic– Cross-pollinating	Easy	Only let one variety go to seed. If stored in a dry place, harvested seeds can be used for planting. To produce more seeds, separate the plants that will be harvested for leaves from those that will be harvested for seeds.
Dill	Annual– Hermaphroditic– Cross-pollinating	Easy	Only cultivate one variety. If stored in a dry place, harvested seeds can be used for planting. To produce more seeds, separate the plants that will be harvested for leaves from those that will be harvested for seeds.
Gherkin	Annual– Monoecious– Cross-pollinating	Medium	Hybridizes with cucumber but not with squash, zucchini, or melon. Only cultivate one variety. Alternatively, use hand pollination or an isolation cage.

Seed type	Flower and pollination type	Level of difficulty	Precautions
Parsley, flat- and curly-leaf	Biennial–Hermaphroditic–Cross-pollinating	Easy	Only let one variety go to seed or use an isolation cage. To produce more seeds, grow one crop for leaves and the other for seeds.
Spring onion	Perennial–Hermaphroditic–Cross-pollinating	Medium	Only let one variety go to seed. Interhybridizes with onions but not with chives or leeks.

Choosing the right varieties

Most vegetables and herbs come in a number of varieties, and each one is slightly different. Choosing between them all is not easy. You will have to make your choice based on a mixture of your own taste criteria and gardening needs: appearance, flavor, vigor, productivity, growth rate, suitability for staggered planting, regularity of behavior from one year to the next, sensitivity or resistance to parasites, etc.

Wild variety

A few less common vegetables like miner's lettuce, fig-leaf gourd, caigua, vila-vila, pepino, and root chervil only exist in one variety: the one that exists in nature. This is known as the "wild variety." Since their seeds require no special precautions when being removed, they are undoubtedly the easiest to harvest.

What about F1 hybrids?

If you want to produce your own seeds, choosing varieties becomes even pricklier. Many varieties that are cultivated today—including organic ones—are F1 hybrids which, for genetic reasons, cannot propagate through normal reproduction. The majority of recent tomato, pepper, eggplant, cucumber, zucchini, sweet corn, and melon varieties grown today are F1 hybrids. Other vegetables, however, like lettuce, frisée and escarole, mâche, leeks, Fabaceae (peas, beans, lentils, chickpeas), as well as the great majority of herbs, resist being cultivated as hybrids. For celery, turnips, carrots, beets, radishes, and onions, open pollinated (reproducible) seed varieties are still the norm, but F1 alternatives exist (though they are of little interest in a family garden). For artichokes, squash, cabbage, and asparagus, the tendency has reversed in recent years and traditional varieties have become a minority. An even bigger problem is that certain crops like forced endives, mini cucumbers, and Napa cabbage are only found as F1 hybrids. You will run into the same issue if you want to grow large, good-looking heads of broccoli. F1 gherkins produce only female flowers that develop into fruit without needing fertilization, and they are distinctly more productive than traditional varieties—this is a fact. But while these non-reproducible cultivars may be tempting, you will have to buy new seeds to sow every year . . . which is a bit problematic if you're trying to be self-sufficient!

THOSE DARN F1S!

F1 hybrids are often unwelcome guests in a garden designed to be self-sufficient. These hybrids are produced by crossing two stable varieties (varieties that, after self-fertilizing, produce plants identical to the parents) and their seeds obey Mendel's first law, which states that the first generation will be uniform. The problem is that seeds from the second generation reactivate the characteristics of their grandparent plants and only display certain traits of their parent plants. Moral of the story: if you sow seeds from F1 plants, you never know what you'll get!

Because its seeds never reproduce identically, the F1 Lipari pepper cannot last in a self-sufficient garden—what a shame!

Limiting your options . . .

If you want to produce your own seeds and not use F1 hybrids, your list of options becomes even shorter. You will have to choose from a list of open pollinated varieties that are in the public domain. It is hard to find varieties these days that are truly "local," which makes those that are all the more precious. These varieties are often a closely guarded secret, kept alive by passionate gardeners. If these gardeners have no one to "inherit" their seeds, those varieties will disappear with them.

It will take several years of trying things out to discover your own gardening style and the best plant varieties for your land. You are going to have pleasant and unpleasant surprises. The following list proposes a few tried and true open pollinated varieties of each garden crop.

→ VEGETABLE VARIETIES

Vegetable	Varieties
Artichoke	Cardoon and Imperial Star (Atlantic and Mediterranean climate)
Arugula	Cultivated and wild varieties (Diplotaxis)
Asparagus	Purple Passion, and Mary Washington
Bean, bush	Extra thin to thin: Maxi, Triomphe de Farcy, and Aiguillon Yellow: Fructidor Purple: Velour Flat Green: Nassau Flat Yellow: Capitano Other varieties: Coco nain blanc précoce, Cocagne, Flambo, Pactol, Lingot (Swiss white), and Wonder
Bean, fava	Aguadulce
Bean, pole	Green: Cobra, Reine du Neckar, and Fortex Purple: Blauhilde Yellow: Golden Gate Other varieties: Alaric, Soissons gros blanc, and Coco Sophie
Beet, red	Crapaudine, Burpee's Golden, Forono, De Chioggia, and Albina Vereduna
Bok choy	Prize Choy and Pak Choï de Shanghai
Broccoli, calabrese	Waltham
Brussels sprouts	Groninger
Cabbage, head	Green Mariner and January King
Cabbage, Napa	Michihilli
Cabbage, red	Kalibos and Red Acre
Cabbage, Savoy	Chieftan Savoy
Cabbages, various Asian	Chijimisai and Green Tatsoi
Carrot	Little Finger, St. Valery, New Kuroda
Cauliflower, summer and fall	Odysseus
Celery	D'Elne and Utah Tall
Celery root	Ibis and Prinz
Chard	Fordhook Giant, Barese, and Perpetual
Chickpea	Any heirloom variety
Chicory, wild	Sugarloaf and Uranus
Cucumber	Dar Tanja, and Marketmore
Dandelion	Italiko rosso and French Dandelion

Vegetable	Varieties
Eggplant	Black Beauty, Diamond, Kamo, and Listada de Gandia
Endive	Salad King
Escarole, summer and fall	Batavian Full Heart
Fennel	Florence
Frisée, summer and fall	Heirloom Frisée
Kale	Westlandse Winter
Kale, red Russian	Red Russian
Kohlrabi	Dyna, Noriko, and Superschmeltz
Leek	Autumn Giant, Bulgarian Giant, and Carentan Leek
Lentil	Flora
Lettuce, cutting	Red Ruffled Oak, Blush Butter Cos, and Sucrine
Lettuce, head, spring	Bergam's Green and Nancy
Lettuce, head, summer and fall	Buttercrunch and Kagraner Sommer Lettuce
Lettuce, head, winter	Ice Queen, Salanova
Mâche	Any heirloom variety
Melon and watermelon	Melon: Charentais, Golden Honeymoon, Sweet Passion Watermelon: Crimson Sweet and Sugar Baby
Miner's lettuce	Wild variety
Onion, spring harvest	He Shi Ko and Ishikura
Onion, storage	Australian Brown Onion and Yellow Sweet Spanish
Orache	Aurora and Blonde
Parsnip	Demi-long de Guernesey and Mitra
Peas	Petit Provençal and Douce Provence
Pepper	Yolo Wonder, Petit Marseillais, Doux des Landes, Lipstick, Pusztagold, Orange Bell, and Yellow Monster
Physalis peruviana	Wild variety
Purslane	Green Purslane
Radicchio	Chioggia: Indigo, Leonardo, and Palla Rossa Others: Castelfranco, Grumolo Verde, Rouge de Trévise, and Rouge de Vérone
Radish, spring	Round: Raxe, Topsi, Gaudry, Zlata, Malaga, and Sniezka Semi-long: Nelson, Patricia, and Pernot Long: Ostergruss and Glaçon
Radish, summer, fall, and winter	Misato Rose, Misato Green, Rose d'hiver de Chine, and Pink Beauty

Vegetable	Varieties
Rutabaga	Wilhelmsburger and American Purple Top
Sorrel	Large de Belleville and Sanguine
Spinach	Matador (Viking) and Géant d'hiver
Squash, various, including turban squash, red kuri squash, and pumpkin	Butternut-Orange, Uchiki Kuri, Rouge d'Étampes, and Atlantic Giant
Sweet corn	Golden Bantam
Tomato	Rose de Berne, Pêche rose, Grosse plate du Portugal, Green Zebra, Goldene Königin, Persimmon, Indigo Blue, Andine cornue, Black Cherry, Gold Nugget, Sweet Baby, Délice du jardinier, Poire jaune, and Poire rouge
Turnip, fall	Hakurai
Turnip, purple top Milan	Oceanic and Purple Top White Globe
Winter squash	Musquée de Provence, Sucrine du Berry, and Early Butternut
Zucchini and pattypan squash	Zucchini: Black Beauty, Genovese, Ronde de Nice, and Rheinau Gold Pattypan squash: Croblan, Orange, and Panaché vert et blanc

Most purslane varieties will happily self-seed.

→ HERB VARIETIES

Herb	Varieties
Basil	Grand vert, Fin vert, Marseilles Lemon, Réglisse, and Freddy
Bay leaf	Wild variety
Chervil	Simple and Frisé
Chili pepper	Cayenne, D'Espelette, and De Bresse
Chives	Polyvit and Twiggy
Cilantro	Wild variety and Lemon
Dill	Wild variety, Dukat Goldkrone, and Tetra Gold
Gherkin	Fin de Meaux and Amélioré de Bourbonne
Lavender	English lavender (Lavandula angustifolia)
Lovage	Wild variety
Parsley, curly- and flat-leaf	Flat-leaf: Géant d'Italie and Hamburger Schnitt Curly-leaf: Favorit
Spring onion	Blanche hâtive and Red Welch

Harvesting and storing seeds

Seed harvesting takes place between June and September. All fruit should be picked as late as possible to ensure that the seeds are fully ripe. The stems from podded or headed plants (like beans and onions) can be clipped off and placed in a small crate lined with a sheet of paper before being stored somewhere warm and dry (but not in direct sunlight). Once the pods or heads are totally dry, use your fingers to shell and clean the seeds, then transfer them to labeled bags. Fruiting vegetables with pulp should be allowed to ripen until they are no longer edible. To harvest the seeds, cut the fruit into pieces and separate the seeds from the pulp before gently washing them in water. Spread them out on a paper towel to dry in the shade somewhere fairly warm (at least 64°F to 68°F [18°C to 20°C]). Once dry—this will probably take fifteen days—remove the seeds from the paper towel and place them in bags labeled by variety. Your seeds will last longest if you store them in a cool, dry place.

6
CULTIVATING YOUR GARDEN AND STARTING SEEDLINGS

If you save your seeds and produce your own seedlings, you will no longer be tied down by the range and availability of varieties offered by seed manufacturers and retailers. You will also limit the very real risk of introducing parasites to your garden that might be present on young plants sold by your local horticulturist. Growing seeds in the garden and starting seedlings go hand in hand: each one is necessary for the other.

Direct-seeding

Direct-seeding allows you to harvest vegetables and herbs from the very spot where they were planted. This is the best option for crops that germinate and grow quickly like radishes, purslane, and Asian cabbages that are harvested as young shoots. It is also a good idea for crops like carrots, beans, and turnips that will not tolerate transplanting.

Seeds should be planted in well-aerated loose soil and can either be scattered over an entire area or planted in rows (spacing will depend on the crop). Make sure not to sow too many seeds close together and do not plant them at a depth more than one to two times their size. One heavy watering is usually enough to press the soil down after planting.

Direct-seeded crops usually need one manual weeding and clearing early on to suppress any unwanted seedlings.

Peas, green beans, fava beans, lentils, and chickpeas are planted in rows.

Vegetables to direct-seed	Herbs to direct-seed
Carrot, various Asian cabbages including bok choy, miner's lettuce, endive, spinach, fava bean, pole bean, bush bean, cutting lettuce, lentil, mâche, sweet corn, turnip (fall), turnip (purple top Milan), onion, parsnip, pea, dandelion, chickpea, purslane, radish (spring and summer), radish (summer, fall, and winter), arugula, rutabaga	Dill, basil, chervil, spring onion, chives, cilantro, gherkin, curly-leaf parsley, flat-leaf parsley

Direct-seed or transplant?

In practice, most vegetables can "technically" be direct-seeded. This is the case for chard, red beets, kohlrabi, kale, Napa cabbage, chicories, cucumbers, zucchini and pattypan squash, various other squash, melon, and watermelon. But for multiple reasons—the ability to get a head start on seedlings in a sheltered area, easily tend to them, limit weed invasion, compensate for a lack of space in the garden, etc.—many gardeners prefer to plant seeds in trays before transplanting them in the garden. Here I have, for example, suggested direct-seeding bok choy, sweet corn, onions, dandelions, arugula, and rutabaga, but they can also be transplanted after the seed gets its start in a tray cell. In the same way, basil, spring onion, chives, and parsley are not always planted using direct-seeding and do just fine if they are sown in trays and transplanted instead. The results do not differ significantly and whatever method saves you the most time is best.

Transplanting with soil blocks

After being seeded in trays, many vegetables are ready to be transplanted in soil blocks after three to five weeks of growth.

Vegetables to transplant using soil blocks	Herbs to transplant using soil blocks
Chard, red beet, Calabrese broccoli, celery, celery root, frisée (summer and fall), radicchio, wild chicory, escarole (summer and fall), Brussels sprouts, green and red head cabbage, kale, Savoy cabbage, cauliflower (summer and fall), bok choy, Napa cabbage, kohlrabi, spinach, fennel, head lettuce, sweet corn, sorrel, dandelion, leek, purslane, arugula, rutabaga	Dill, basil, chives, cilantro, curly-leaf parsley, flat-leaf parsley

Planting in small soil blocks lets you wait for the best weather conditions before transplanting the young seedlings you started indoors.

Seeding a tray

Planting seeds in a tray or flat can be done in as many different ways as there are seeds. Large seeds that can be handled easily like chard, red beet, sweet corn, and Cucurbitaceae are planted one at a time, while small seeds from parsley, arugula, and purslane plants are deposited in pinches of five to ten seeds. Cabbage, lettuce, and chicory seeds can be planted in threes and reduced to a single plant after seedlings have pierced the soil.

1 Fill the trays with a light, aerated substrate.

2. Tap the bottom of the tray against a table to compact the soil.

3. Use a pencil to make a hole in each block or plug where your seed(s) will go.

4. Depending on the crop, place the seeds one or several at a time in the small cavities you have created (some particularly tiny seeds like purslane and celery are simply placed on top of the substrate).

5. Pat down the soil and water using a fine spray nozzle.

6. Keep the tray damp until the seedlings break through the soil.

7. Clear away any unwanted seedlings and only preserve the most vigorous seedling in each block.

8. After a few weeks, the young seedlings develop a vigorous root system. Remove the soil blocks or plugs from the tray by pressing your finger against the base and plant them in the ground.

Starting seedlings indoors

Seedlings are best started in a shelter like a cold frame whose only heat source is the "greenhouse effect." Start your indoor arugula and lettuce plantings in February, but wait until March for the first big wave of spring seed planting (tomato, eggplant, pepper, celery) and early April for the second wave (zucchini, squash, cucumber, melon). A warm layer of decomposing organic matter—though not a necessity—may help make sure young plants are ready in time for transplanting, which is usually the first two weeks in May. In the event of negative outdoor temperatures, you will need to cover your sheltered seedlings with one or two frost blankets.

Repotting seedlings before planting them in the garden

Repotting seedlings only needs to be done for a few crops, but they happen to be ones that are essential in any garden: tomato, eggplant, pepper, squash, zucchini, cucumber, melon, and basil. You can repot these crops in a cold shelter when the first true leaves appear.

DIRECT-SEEDING IN POTS

Direct-seeding in pots is often seen as the ideal method for starting squash, zucchini, and cucumbers. Personally, I find that planting in trays and then repotting the seedlings is more practical and not necessarily more time-consuming. Most importantly, it takes up less room when plants are small at a time of year (April) when space indoors is at a premium.

Vegetables to repot before planting in the garden	Herbs to repot before planting in the garden
Artichoke, eggplant, cucumber, Physalis peruviana, zucchini and pattypan squash, winter squash, turban squash, red kuri squash and pumpkin, melon and watermelon, pepper, tomato	Basil, lovage, chili pepper

Tomato plants require one or two repottings before being planted in the garden in May.

73

Propagation by division and cuttings

Perennial kale and sweet potatoes are the only vegetables you should propagate using cuttings. Herbs, on the other hand, are often grown using a process called division. New potatoes and Jerusalem artichokes, which are both grown from tubers, can be propagated using a rather interesting layering technique instead. Division should take place preferably when the vegetative stage begins, whereas cuttings are best taken in summer. Growing garlic and shallots involves yet another method: the cloves of each bulb are separated and placed directly in the ground. This should be done between November and January for purple garlic, between January and March for white garlic, and in March or April for pink garlic and shallots, with the exception of the gray shallot, which is planted in the fall.

Young sweet potato slips require warm temperatures and should not be transplanted before mid-May.

HOW TO PROPAGATE YOUR SWEET POTATOES . . .

Set aside three to five nice-looking tubers somewhere dry at 66°F (19°C) for the entire winter. At the end of February or in early March, transfer them to a vase filled with 1 to 2 inches (3 to 5 cm) of water in a warm place (between 77°F and 82°F [25°C and 28°C]). When the shoots that appear on the tubers reach 4 inches (10 cm) in length, cut them and let these "slips" grow roots in a glass of water. When the first rootlets appear, repot the slips in a sheltered area. Plant them in the garden at the end of May or in June.

Vegetables propagated from cuttings or tubers	Herbs propagated by cuttings or division
Perennial kale, sweet potato, potato, Jerusalem artichoke	Garlic, chives, shallot, tarragon, lovage, lemon balm, mint, oregano, rhubarb, rosemary, sage, stevia, tansy, thyme, lemon thyme, lemon verbena

Replanting your harvested potatoes

In the fall, look through the potatoes you harvested two months ago and collect any tubers that are 1 to 1.5 inches (3 to 4 cm) long. Keep them somewhere cool—in a hole-in the-ground root cellar, for example—until late December to prevent early germination. In January, lay the tubers flat in crates and place the crates in a sunny spot at 60°F/64°F (16°C/18°C). Do not stack them.

When the first buds appear, move the tubers somewhere colder but still well-lit (50°F/59°F [10°C/15°C]) until it is time to plant them in the garden, which should be between mid-April for early varieties and June for late varieties.

Varieties with large tubers and high yields like Charlotte, Mona Lisa, and Pompadour can be collected for several years in a row, but others with low yields and small tubers like Chérie and Ratte will need new slips every three years because of their sensitivity to viral diseases.

Nine months of gardening

Whether you are sowing seeds and transplanting plants in a covered area or outside, you are going to be incredibly busy from February to October. To make tending your garden easier and to save time, group crops together based on their needs, timing, cultivation practices, etc.

Even though this is not possible for crops like leeks, sweet potatoes, and cipollini onions because each one has its own unique needs and way of growing in the garden, many other crops can be planted together. Tomatoes, eggplants, peppers, and Cucurbitaceae, for example, can all be seeded in trays around the same time (April for Cucurbitaceae, March for the rest). If the weather is good, March is also the perfect time to plant seeds for seasonal carrots, spring radishes, and peas directly in the ground. Planting these crops together will allow you to consolidate your work in the garden until the first cool fall temperatures.

Legend: ■ = dark shading, ▨ = light shading

	J	F	M	A	M	J	J	A	S	O	N	D
Fava bean, orache, parsnip		▨										
Asian cabbages and arugula to harvest as shoots		■	▨						■	▨		
White garlic, shallot, pearl onion			■									
Tomato, eggplant, pepper, and chili pepper			▨	■								
Lettuce			■	▨	■	▨	■	▨				
Celery root, celery, sorrel			■		▨	■						
Chard, beet			■	▨	■	■						
Leek						■	■					
Spring radish, arugula, seasonal carrot, peas			▨									
Parsley, flat- and curly-leaf			■		▨	■	▨	■				
Pointed cabbage, broccoli, summer cauliflower, fennel			▨	■								
Dill and cilantro			■	▨								
Early/midseason potato				■								
Cucumber, zucchini, squash, melon, watermelon, sweet corn, basil				▨								
Sweet potato				■	▨	■						
Fall green and red head cabbage, Brussels sprouts, Savoy cabbage, kale				▨	■	■						
Summer frisée and escarole					■							
Storage potato					■	■						
Gherkin					■	▨						
Bean, lentil, chickpea					▨	▨						
Summer radish						▨						

	J	F	M	A	M	J	J	A	S	O	N	D
Sage, hyssop, curry, thyme, lemon thyme, rosemary, tarragon, lavender, lemon balm, mint, stevia, lemon verbena (to be planted in the garden the following spring)						■	■	■				
Spring onion, chives, lovage (to be planted in the garden the following spring)						■	■					
Endive, radicchio (Rouge de Trévise), wild chicory, and dandelion to be forced indoors, winter carrots						■	■					
Fall frisée and escarole, radicchio, sugarloaf chicory, Napa cabbage, bok choy							■	■	■			
Fall turnip, fall and winter radish, rutabaga, mâche, spinach								■	■			
Cipollini onion								■				
Miner's lettuce, root chervil, chervil, arugula									■			
Purple garlic, gray shallot										■	■	

- Seed tray indoors
- Repot indoors
- Direct-seed indoors
- Take cuttings indoors
- Direct-seed in garden
- Plant in garden

PARSLEY ALL YEAR LONG

Your first parsley plantings can turn yellow easily. If you want to harvest this herb from January to December, make sure you plant seeds three times: the March planting will give you a summer harvest, seeds planted in June will produce a fall crop, and the August planting will give you enough to last through the winter until the end of spring the following year.

A lettuce for every season

Lettuce plantings continue nonstop from February (spring cultivars) to October (winter cultivars). You should count on waiting three to four weeks after planting seeds to have small plants ready to plant in the garden. Allow the same amount of time for your young transplants to grow round and ready to harvest. To ensure continuous harvests, each transplanting should be followed by a new round of seeding. Remember to choose the appropriate variety for each time of year.

IN THE GARDEN FOR TWELVE MONTHS—OR MORE!

Perpetual leek seeds are planted in trays indoors in March before the previous year's leek harvest has ended (it is not unheard of to pick the last leeks in May). After being repotted in May, they are finally planted in the garden in June for harvesting beginning in October.

Propagating fruit trees and bushes

There's no need to sow seeds to propagate fruit-bearing trees and bushes! Bushes can be propagated by cuttings—and possibly by layering—and trees can be propagated by grafting, except for the fig tree which should have cuttings taken in the spring just as its leaves appear. Use these three techniques to propagate fruit trees and bushes that are already in your garden or to introduce vigorous varieties growing around the neighborhood. Don't hesitate to ask: no one will say no to giving you a few cuttings or rootstock from a tree or bush growing in their yard.

Even though it is a tree, the fig tree is propagated using cuttings. →

How to take fruit bush cuttings

Summer is the best time to take cuttings. Luckily for you, the garden will not require as much of your attention between June and August. You can use trays with deep holes and the same garden soil you use for planting seeds. If it looks a little too fibrous and moist—which means it is retaining too much water—add some coarse sand without exceeding the 1:5 ratio. The steps outlined below can also be used to propagate bushy herbs like thyme and sage.

1 Select several young stems 4 inches (10 cm) in length. Depending on the plant, you can either trim terminal shoots or cut off a whole branch to section into several cuttings.

2. Trim the base of the cutting just below a knot and remove any lower leaves.

3. Fill your tray with soil and push one cutting into each hole.

4. Water the tray to make the soil stick to the buried part of your cutting.

5. Place the tray in the shade somewhere warm and humid (between 68°F and 77°F [20°C and 25°C]). If temperatures get too high, cover the tray with a moist veil and keep it damp.

6. Depending on the plant, roots may take between fifteen days and two months to appear.

7. Repot when the young roots have filled the hole.

8. Plant your cuttings in the garden the following spring.

An even easier way . . .

Red currant and black currant can also be propagated from hardwood cuttings. In winter, just cut stems 12 inches (30 cm) in length and push them four-fifths of the way into the ground. They will sprout leaves at the end of the following spring, but you will have to wait two years for their first fruits.

Plan B: Layering

Successfully propagating from cuttings involves a kind of race against the clock that depends on the cutting's ability to survive without roots and the appearance of new rootlets that will allow it to start a new life. Cuttings from hard-to-root plants like hazelnut, shadbush, and kiwi, for instance, sometimes die before they produce new roots. Layering allows young plants to grow roots before they are separated from the mother plant and is a less uncertain process. It is usually done using a young branch from the previous year and preferably in the spring.

1 Select a long, pliable branch at the base of the plant you want to propagate.

2. Bend it toward the ground and use a billhook to cut two horizontal notches in the section that will be in the ground.

3. Dig a trench 6 inches (15 cm) deep and lay the branch in it. The tip of the branch should be sticking out of the soil. If you need to, use a U-shaped pin to hold it in place.

4. Refill the hole with a mixture of equal parts topsoil and garden soil. Pat down firmly.

5. Place a stake to help the young branch grow vertically and water the soil.

6. In fall or the following spring, cut the branch behind the roots and pull up the new plant before replanting it in its final home.

Layering a red currant bush will give you a vigorous young plant in the spring.

How to graft fruit trees

Grafting allows you to propagate one tree variety by fusing a piece from one of its branches (known as the scion) onto another tree (the rootstock). There are many ways to do this, but the easiest (and the one most likely to be successful) is shield budding, also known as T-budding. This summer grafting technique works for all fruits with seeds or stones.

Fruit trees are typically shield budded in summer.

1 Select a hardwood branch from the tree you wish to propagate.

2. Clip off any leaves on the scion but leave a short stub of each petiole. Make half-inch (1 cm) slices above and below the bud you want to use for your graft.

3. At the site of your future graft, use a cloth to wipe off any dirt on the rootstock.

4. Make a T-shaped cut in the rootstock and open the two side flaps with the blunt end of a grafting knife to form a pouch.

5. Firmly hold the scion in your left hand if you are right-handed and in your right hand if you are left-handed. Use your grafting knife to peel the bud shield away from the scion branch (the bud shield is the oval-shaped section of bark surrounding the bud).

6. Remove any excess wood attached to the inside of the bud shield (if this wood is not removed, the young shoot will not be able to adhere later).

7. Slide the bud shield into the pouch you created earlier. Hold the bud shield flaps against the rootstock and tightly wrap the graft above and below the bud (traditionally this used to be done with raffia, but today many professionals prefer to use thin strips of rubber secured with a staple).

8. You will know the graft has taken if, after ten days, the petiole stub falls off on its own or when you press it with your finger. The bud itself should still look fresh.

Where to find rootstock

Shield budding requires a scion from the fruit tree you want to propagate, but you will also need a rootstock. Preferences for rootstock can vary from region to region depending on the climate and nature of the soil. A phone call to a nursery in your area will tell you what most people use, and you can place orders in the fall with a local nursery or online. This is the most practical solution if you do not need large quantities (which is usually the case). Rootstock trees grown from seeds—plum trees, sweet cherry trees, peach trees, apple trees, pear trees, etc.—are some of the easiest trees to propagate in a self-sufficient garden. If their seeds are planted in the fall they will be ready for grafting in two or three years, depending on their vigor. Certain trees also send up shoots at the base of the trunk that can be removed and replanted. These can be grafted the summer after planting.

Wedge grafting is done in spring.

7
KEEPING CHICKENS

The garden and the chicken coop work together. Chickens enjoy vegetable peelings, leftover pasta and salad, cheese rinds, and other kitchen waste, and in exchange they remove moss from the lawn as they walk around the yard. In the orchard, they'll gladly devour the larvae of many different insect pests, and last but certainly not least, they offer an excellent source of garden manure all year long.

Chicken coop components

Chickens don't ask for very much: they need a henhouse for the night, an enclosed area (or run) to protect them from predators, and open space—usually the yard—where they can run around and peck at things to eat.

The henhouse

The henhouse is a place for hens to sleep, lay eggs, and, at times, to sit on those eggs until they hatch. Whether you adapt an existing structure or build one specifically for this purpose, its size will depend on the number of chickens you plan on adopting. It should be easy to access, protected from rain, humidity, and strong wind, and easy to clean. It should also have roosts and include nesting boxes for three hens. An egg access door on the outside of the henhouse will make it easier for you to collect eggs. Cover the floor with a litter of straw and change it regularly.

A small 24 x 16 inch (60 x 40 cm) henhouse can house up to four hens.

Chicken run

The chicken run is a sort of meeting place for your hens where they are protected from predators and have access to food and water. If your run is entirely screened-in—and hopefully it is—you will be able to keep an eye on your guests, which will be helpful when it comes time for them to mate. Since hens are less afraid of winter cold than extreme summer heat, make sure part of the run is in the shade. The litter of straw you keep on the ground combined with the chicken waste will become your source of manure.

HOMEMADE GUANO

Guano is seabird excrement that is rich in nitrogen, phosphorous, and potassium. Chicken manure is nothing to sneeze at, though—it's rich in minerals, too! Diluted in water, it makes an excellent organic fertilizer, especially for potted plants. If you prefer to use it mixed in with straw from the coop litter, it makes an invaluable homemade manure for your garden.

What about ducks?

Indian Runner ducks are easy to recognize thanks to their almost vertical posture and are very popular among permaculture enthusiasts. The female ducks are good layers, efficient consumers of slugs, and will do very little damage to a yard. What's more, ducks are perfectly happy living with chickens. If you have a backyard measuring 700 square yards (a little less than ¼ acre) and already have six hens and one rooster, you should be able to adopt two to three female ducks and one drake.

How many henhouses do I need?

While you can certainly build your own henhouse, there are plenty of chicken house kits on the market. Choose one suitable for the number of chickens you have but also keep in mind that you will at times need to isolate a hen that is broody, injured, or sick. One or two small henhouses to support the main structure will give you options for handling all kinds of situations.

Free-range space

Open space gives your chickens the freedom to forage over a wide area. A grassy orchard or a yard with trees and bushes would work perfectly (hens do too much damage to a vegetable garden to allow them to walk around there freely during the growing season). The chicken run and free-range space should meet your flock's needs for outdoor space. While the run is relatively small—19 to 30 square yards (16 to 25 square meters) for around ten chickens—when it comes to free-range space, each chicken should be allotted a *minimum* of 24 square yards (20 square meters). To prevent your chickens from rambling too far, free-range space should be surrounded by a wall or fence that is tall and sturdy. Plan for a height of about 2 yards (2 meters) for light breeds, and less than 1.5 yards (1.5 meters) for heavy breeds. Chickens can be allowed to roam freely between the henhouse and the run, but access to free-range space should be monitored—it is up to you to decide what time of day the chickens get to enjoy it.

HOW MUCH FREE-RANGE TIME SHOULD I GIVE MY CHICKENS?

Your hens should be allowed to free range on a regular basis, but don't leave them out there all the time. In the morning, keep them in the run with access to the henhouse so you won't have to go hunting all over your yard for eggs—Easter should only come once a year! Hens typically lay their eggs between 10:00 a.m. and 2:00 p.m. and usually in the same place. Ducks, on the other hand, will lay wherever they feel like it.

Make sure your hens always have enough clean water available.

Food and drink

Now that your hens have a place to live, it's time to take care of them! They should always have plenty to eat and drink: their well-being, health, and laying regularity depend on it. Remember that food and water consumption are inversely proportional: when temperatures rise in summer, food needs decrease while water demands increase. And the reverse happens when the temperature drops in winter!

Water

Hens usually drink a quantity of water that is twice the amount of feed they eat, which adds up to roughly ¾ to 1 gallon (3 to 4 liters) of water for a flock of eight to ten chickens. The water should be changed frequently in summer because ingesting algae is harmful to chickens' health. In winter, regularly pour hot water into the waterer to melt any ice.

A chicken waterer with legs and a water container is easy to refill and will help you keep the water clean. There are many different kinds available (fountain, cup, barrel, etc.) in both plastic and metal. Waterers with nipples are another clean option. They do not waste water and will work well for chickens or any poultry that drink small quantities very often. Nipple waterers are usually equipped with a water reserve of 3 gallons (12 liters) and are installed 16 inches (40 cm) from the ground on the chicken run frame. If you have around ten hens, a waterer this size will give you fresh water for three or four days at a time. Use well or tap water and avoid rainwater that has been collected in barrels.

Chicken feed

Hens are omnivores (they eat what you eat) and have a sense of smell similar to ours. Unlike ducks, though, they are primarily granivores and should always have a mixture of grains available including wheat, triticale, barley, whole oats, and cracked corn, the last of which should make up less than a third of the total feed ration. Chickens also enjoy field peas (up to 15 percent of the mixture), and oilseeds like sunflower, rapeseed, and soybeans (no more than 5 percent of the mixture). Use the same mixture every time because chickens tend to dislike change.

It is not always easy to plant the amount of grain you need to feed your chickens, if only because of the amount of space required. In rural and suburban areas, many farmers offer a good price for quality feed mixes. Plan for between 9 and 11 pounds (4 and 5 kg) of grain per chicken per month. Pour your grain mixture into an anti-waste hopper feeder that you can refill once all the grain

has been eaten. A reserve of 44 pounds (20 kg) will feed a flock of around ten chickens for fifteen days. Like the waterer, the feeder should be set up inside the chicken run, but do not place the two next to each other or you run the risk of accidentally getting your grain wet while filling the waterer.

Chickens should always have access to a mixture of clean, dry grains.

While grains make up most of a chicken's diet, they won't say no to leafy greens.

Cabbage, spinach, chard, weeds, and more

Chickens love greens from the garden. Lettuces that have gone to seed, cabbage leaves, spinach, and chard are some of their favorites. In a self-sufficient kitchen garden, you will have plenty of these in summer and winter. There are few plants that chickens will not eat and they also enjoy weeds like chickweed (hence the name), goosefoots, groundsel, shepherd's purse, amaranth, nettles (leave them out to dry for a day and they will lose their sting), and foxtails (these will always be popping up through your mulch and chickens devour them as soon as they pull them out of the ground).

A vegetable is rarely consumed in its entirety, no matter what kind it is. Sometimes, as is the case with cauliflower, the part consumed is much smaller than the part to "throw out." Chickens will gladly eat any of these vegetable leftovers if you put them in the run, along with other kitchen waste like fish, shellfish, meat scraps, dairy products . . . and eggshells (if they are crushed first). Excess winter root vegetables like red beets, turnips, and Jerusalem artichokes should be pureed beforehand.

How many chickens?

Five to eight hens will provide enough eggs for a family of four. A rooster is not a must-have for egg-laying but is necessary for breeding.

Eggs every day

Depending on the breed and the time of year, a hen lays between 3 and 6 eggs per week, or 150 to 300 eggs a year. Multiply these numbers by the number of hens you want in your yard and you will see this is more than enough, especially since whole eggs in their shells can be kept in the refrigerator for at least five weeks without any noticeable decrease in quality. Hens lay the most eggs between February and May, slightly less in the summer and even less in the fall before picking up the pace little by little in December. Young hens are considered ready to lay between sixteen and twenty weeks, but the exact timing depends on the breed and some hens do not lay their first egg until they are seven or eight months old.

Growing your flock

Purebred hens will lay properly for three years (red hens and other farm chicken breeds do most of their laying between five and eighteen months after being born). If you want to make sure some of your guests are always laying eggs, you will need to expand your flock! Adding a rooster is the key to getting your eggs to hatch.

Do I need a rooster?

Having a rooster does not influence the quality of egg-laying or the quantity of eggs your hens produce. If your goal is collecting fresh eggs for eating, its presence is entirely optional. If you want to have chicks, though, you will need a rooster.

Choosing chicken breeds

If you have your heart set on a specific breed, do some research about how many eggs it lays in a year, how broody its hens are, and everything that sets it apart from other breeds. If none of its particularities seem prohibitive, go ahead! Otherwise, get information about other breeds that might better suit your needs.

Whatever breed you choose, give priority to heavy breeds (between 6.5 and 7.5 lbs (3 and 3.5 kg) for hens and between 7.5 and 8.5 lbs (3.5 and 4 kg) for roosters). These breeds are better producers both in terms of the number and the size of their eggs. Incidentally, their weight also prevents them from perching in trees at night or fluttering into your neighbor's yard. Heavy roosters are also calmer than lighter breeds and have a softer crow (though there are exceptions, of course). It should also be noted that some large hens like the Cochin and the Brahma are raised for their ornamental qualities as opposed to their level of egg production. In the United States, popular laying breeds include Australorp, Barred Plymouth Rock, Buff Orpington, Rhode Island Red, Golden Comet, Ameraucana, Golden Laced Wyandottes, Leghorn, Speckled Sussex, and New Hampshire Red.

Bielefelder

Orpington

As if choosing chicken breeds wasn't hard enough, remember that most breeds also come in several different colors. A breed's overall shape, caliber, and characteristics have nothing to do with their plumage, of course—this is a purely aesthetic choice! While the number of breeds is fairly stable, varieties with new colors continue to appear regularly.

A GOOD PLACE TO START

If you're having a hard time deciding, keep things simple: get yourself a rooster and four to five Speckled Sussex hens. They are hardy, lay well, and are good brooders. This well-known breed is not very demanding and will not disappoint.

Black Copper Marans hen

Géline de Touraine hen

Salmon Faverolle hen

93

Your guests will love a grassy free-range area because it gives them a place to peck at grass, scratch the ground, and nibble on snails and insects.

→ BREEDS FOR A SELF-SUFFICIENT GARDEN

Breed	Varieties	Eggs per year (average)	Egg color	Broodiness	Additional characteristics
Australorp	Black with hints of green	200 eggs	Light brown	Fairly good brooder	Adapts easily to both cold and hot temperatures.
Bielefelder	Salmon golden cuckoo, salmon silver cuckoo	220 eggs	Beige/ brown	Average to mediocre brooder	Female and male chicks can be distinguished at birth. Good winter layer.

Breed	Varieties	Eggs per year (average)	Egg color	Broodiness	Additional characteristics
Belgian malines	Blue-gray cuckoo on white base	180 eggs	Light brown	Average to good brooder	Female and male chicks can be distinguished after hatching (like many cuckoo chickens). Its feathered legs and feet differentiate it from the Coucou de Rennes.
Faverolle	Pale salmon, dark salmon	200 eggs	Beige	Good brooder	The hen and rooster are sometimes raised as ornamental chickens.
Géline de touraine	Black	200 eggs	Dark cream	Good brooder	Good winter layer.
Jersey giant	Black, white, blue	180 eggs	Brown	Average to good brooder	Docile chicken despite its impressive size.
Marans	Silver cuckoo, golden cuckoo, black copper, blue copper, buff, etc.	180 eggs	Chocolate brown	Average to good brooder	Egg color and quantity vary significantly depending on the variety.
New Hampshire	Buff with black tail, buff with blue tail	220 eggs	Brown	Good brooder	Good winter layer.
Orpington	Buff, black, white, blue, tricolor, etc.	180 eggs	Light brown	Good brooder	Eggs are relatively small. Often raised as ornamental chickens.

Breed	Varieties	Eggs per year (average)	Egg color	Broodiness	Additional characteristics
Plymouth rock	Barred, white, buff, partridge, gold-barred, silver-penciled, etc.	200 eggs	Dark yellow	Good brooder	Rapid growth.
Rhode Island	Mahogany	220 eggs	Light brown	Average brooder	The rooster knows how to make itself heard . . .
Sussex	Speckled	220 eggs	Beige	Good brooder	Good winter layer.
Wyandotte	Silver, silver-laced, golden-laced, blue, black, buff, etc.	200 eggs	Beige to brown	Average to good brooder	Egg production, egg color, and brooding instinct vary significantly depending on the variety.

Happy hens

How do you recognize a healthy hen? Well, its feathers are full, shiny, and clean—though they may look stained in rainy weather—because a healthy chicken will groom itself regularly. Its nostrils are dry and free of mucus, its comb and wattles are bright red (this is especially true if a hen is laying), and its anal orifice is clean. The head and tail are erect and in constant motion—chickens are curious and always on the lookout!

Chickens like living together . . .

A hen—or a rooster—will wither if left on its own, but that doesn't mean there won't be a little bit of pecking and infighting to disturb the tranquility of the henhouse. This usually happens while each guest is finding or reestablishing its place in the flock, which is organized around the rooster and the alpha hen.

Watch out for stress!

Chickens are easily frightened and do not like change. They enjoy having a routine for eating and their other daily habits. Anything new, even something intended to improve their comfort level, will perturb them. If a modification must be made (new guests, change of rooster, change in food type, etc.) try to make changes gradually.

Silkie hens are appreciated for their excellent brooding and maternal instincts.

HENHOUSE QUARRELS

Hens peck each other to establish a hierarchy within the group. The alpha hen is the fiercest of all, and unfortunately the weakest hen risks being harassed by the entire flock. Once the hierarchy is in place—usually because the other hens have given up and submitted to the dominant hen—everything returns to normal.

Parasites and illness

Chickens—and ducks, to an even greater extent—are hardy creatures. Their plumage protects them from the cold and an oily secretion protects their feathers from rain (they still like shelter in the event of a long rainstorm, though). Unlike plants, chickens have an efficient immune system that keeps most diseases and parasites in check, but like all living things they are still susceptible to a variety of illnesses. As long as you keep the henhouse in good condition and give them enough space, food, and water, they should only rarely have any health problems.

Use preventative measures

A covered chicken run will protect your hens from disease-carrying wild birds, and an anti-waste feeder should cut down on the number of rodents that could bring other diseases to your flock. Make sure your chickens have clean water and a balanced diet. Feed and water should be available at all times—chickens are perfectly capable of regulating when they eat and you will not overfeed them. They should also have suitable shelter and enough room to peck and scratch the ground.

All of the measures mentioned above will help prevent coccidiosis, a disease brought on by excess moisture that affects the digestive system of young chicks. Make sure wherever chicks are kept—both at birth and as they start to grow—is clean and dry to avoid the costly treatments that this disease requires if it does appear. Marek's disease

A limp, whitish comb is a sign that a hen is in poor health.

Molting

Beginning in their second year of life (generally around eighteen months), hens lose and re-grow their feathers every year between late summer and early winter. They will not be at their most attractive during this time and you may think they are suffering from every disease imaginable. They also lay fewer eggs and sometimes stop laying altogether. Don't worry! Your hen is not sick and this is a natural process to help it prepare for winter. What should you do? Nothing. Wait for it to pass and don't make any changes to your hens' diet, which should continue to be rich in grains even if they have stopped laying eggs.

Chickens like living in groups but also appreciate tranquility and space.

is a common chicken disease that afflicts young birds between three and four months of age. Farms with large flocks use early vaccination to prevent Marek's disease but this is not necessary for backyard chickens. Another disease that flares up on intensive poultry farms where chickens are exposed to prolonged stress (again, not your backyard!) is infectious coryza, which is bacterial in origin and whose primary symptom is nasal discharge.

Change the litter regularly and always put down clean, dry straw. This is rule number one. You should also let your chickens spend as much time as possible out in the fresh air. Buy your first hens from a reputable breeder to avoid introducing disease-carrying birds. Down the road, introduce new birds by buying fertilized eggs from a breeder instead of adult hens—your risk of contamination and disease transmission will be almost nonexistent. Snails are potential intermediate hosts for a variety of intestinal worms, but a small flock of Indian Runner ducks will take care of them. Diversify the greens in your chickens' diet by giving them sprigs of thyme or mint to reinforce their immune systems with something that won't negatively affect intestinal flora. Poultry lice and mites—with the exception of red roost mites, which only a thorough cleaning of the henhouse can conquer—are external parasites that chickens get rid of naturally by "bathing" in dust or sand (mixed with diatomaceous earth, if you have it).

Your first hens

Even in a self-sufficient henhouse, your first guests have to come from somewhere. The question is what to buy: day-old chicks, six- to eight-week-old pullets (young hens), or hens that are ready to lay eggs?

Pullets or hens ready to lay are your best option. Young chicks require special attention whereas pullets are completely independent. If they are born in March or April—meaning you will adopt them in May or June—you can place them directly in your covered chicken run with a feeder filled with age-appropriate feed and a waterer. Put them in the henhouse for the night and let them out in the morning. When night comes, they will find their way back to the henhouse on their own. If it rains during the first few days, check to make sure they have the instinct to seek shelter and keep from getting wet.

Large breed hens that are four or five months old are considered ready to lay. They acclimate easily to new surroundings between May and September and their diet is the same as an adult hen's. You will also have the pleasure of gathering your first eggs within weeks of their arrival. If you have adopted a flock that includes a rooster and five or six hens, breeding can start as soon as the following spring.

WHEN WILL I GET MY FIRST EGG?

Take a look at your hens' combs. Their pale pink color won't stand out very much at first, but they will grow in size and become progressively redder and more serrated. This is the signal that their first egg is on the way!

Creating a sustainable flock

Self-sufficiency in the henhouse depends on the birth of new chicks. But you won't need a fancy incubator or a brooder requiring a lot of electricity—the hen will keep the eggs warm and raise the chicks herself! Just like in the garden, where plants will naturally grow on their own and bear fruit once the seeds or seedlings are planted, your role is simply to provide the flock with the well-being it needs to breed. You don't have to "do" anything for the eggs because the hen takes care of brooding, maintaining humidity levels, turning and airing the eggs, and incubation temperature. After the chicks hatch, she offers them a place to stay warm and teaches them to drink, eat, roost, and seek shelter from the rain, most of which they will learn by mimicking their mother's behavior.

One brood a year . . .

Raising one brood of chicks a year is enough to sustain your flock. If you decide to do more, just make sure you can find enough chicken enthusiasts to take any extra young birds off your hands. Hens born in April or May will start laying in October or early November and continue for two or three years.

. . . for a dozen chicks

If one of your hens starts brooding with around fifteen eggs, you can count on having five to six female chicks and just as many male chicks. Remember that some eggs will not hatch and that not all newborn chicks survive. The henhouse is like the garden—not everything goes the way we want it to!

The hen cares for and protects her chicks until they are six weeks old.

Encouraging a hen to brood

Some hens try to brood two or even three times between March and June, while others show no desire to at all. A broody hen is happy staying in her nest much longer than necessary to lay her egg. If you notice this happening, isolate the hen in a relatively small space and place six to eight plastic eggs in a nest with hay or straw. If she sits right down in her new nest, this is a good sign. Wait one or two days to make sure she still seems interested. Then you can exchange the fake eggs with real eggs you would like her to hatch.

Which eggs should go under the hen?

Fertilized eggs, of course! If you have an established breeding flock with a rooster, just collect your eggs each day and write the date on each egg in pencil. Store at room temperature in an egg crate, point down. Then take the fifteen most recent eggs—they should be less than eight days old—and put them under the broody hen. While the hen takes her daily walk, remove the plastic eggs and place the fertilized eggs in the nest.

   If you have a broody hen but no rooster, you will need to talk to a breeder in your area to get fertilized eggs for the breeds you want to raise. Place the eggs under the hen as soon as you get back to the henhouse just as you would if you were using eggs from your own flock.

HOW CAN I BE SURE A HEN IS BROODY?

A broody hen will huddle over her nest all day. If you reach your hand toward her while she is in the nest, she'll probably puff up her feathers, cackle, and peck at you. But when she leaves the nest to eat or drink—never for more than fifteen minutes—she lets down her feathers and clucks the way she usually does.

What to do with a broody hen when you don't need any chicks

Isolate the hen in a cage somewhere cool and shady and cover the cage with a tarp so the hen is in relative darkness. Give her only vegetables or kitchen leftovers to eat—no seeds! And as much water as she wants, of course. The desire to brood usually disappears after two or three days and then she will start laying again.

When it's time to brood, the hen will make herself a comfortable nest that she will occupy for three weeks.

Brooding

The hen will sit on her eggs day and night for twenty-one days. She will only leave her nest to eat, drink, and poop. As long as her nest is somewhere calm and isolated, a broody hen is totally capable of being on her own during this time. You can let her come and go as she pleases. Some breeders prefer to lock up broody hens and only let them out once a day for fifteen minutes, but this restricts both the breeder and the hen and does not necessarily produce better results.

Hatching

After eighteen or nineteen days, the chicks perforate the air pocket on the large end of the egg. On the twenty-first day, they crack the shell. The wet and trembling newborns dry off quickly thanks to their mother's warmth and are able to move around a few hours after hatching. Still guided by their mother, they drink from the chick waterer that you should have installed nearby and the next day they will peck at the chick starter crumbles in their feeder. You can spoil them occasionally by adding young lettuce leaves, chickweed from the garden, or crushed yolk from a hard-boiled egg.

MALE OR FEMALE?

Statistically, half of your chicks will be female and the other half will be male. Determining a chick's sex can be difficult for a non-professional because it requires an examination of the genital organs inside the cloaca. Most cuckoo breeds (chickens with white feathers patterned with gray or black stripes, in other words) like Malines and other breeds like Bielefelders can be autosexed (distinguished) at birth because male and female chicks are different colors.

Little chicks grow up

If it's in a safe place, keep the chicks wherever the hen had her nest. You can also transfer the hen to a small henhouse and block the entrance. Keep fresh water and chick starter feed available at all times. The mother will pick at this food in the early days to encourage her chicks to do the same. Cover the floor with a thin layer of straw. After ten days, if the weather is warm (above 72°F [22°C]) and it is not raining, place the hen and her chicks in a cage outside during the day (make sure they have somewhere to take shelter if they need to). If the nights are still cool or if rain is in the forecast, bring them back into the henhouse while you wait for

Young chicks require special food adapted to their needs.

conditions to improve. Unless the weather is extremely unusual, chicks born in early May will adapt easily to the outdoor air, but they are unable to regulate their internal

The mother hen nurtures her chicks from the time they hatch until they are at least six weeks old.

temperature until they are three weeks old and their first feathers replace their down. Until then they must be able to stay close to their mother at night or in damp weather.

Chicks stay with their mother for six weeks, at which point she starts laying eggs again and abandons her now independent offspring. They will gradually grow tired of the small pieces of starter feed and move on to adult food (wheat, triticale, rye, barley, cracked corn). Offer them greens like lettuce, chard, and chickweed on a regular basis. Isolate young pullets in a small enclosure inside the chicken run so that older and younger hens can see each other without sharing physical space. After four months, pullets will be eating the same diet as adult hens.

Don't forget to install roosts in the henhouse: chickens
love to be up high, away from potential predators.

A hen's first eggs

Hens truly enter adult life when they begin
laying eggs at around five or six months
(some breeds start a little later). You will
know a hen is almost ready when her comb
reddens and her feathery rump grows larger.

Maintaining your henhouse

Once they're used to their surroundings, hens
require very little supervision. They will go
into the henhouse at night without prompting
and come back out early every morning.
Just take a quick look now and then—when
gathering eggs, for instance—to reassure
yourself that everything is going well. If you
are worried about attacks from predators,
close the henhouse door at night. In a
predator-proof chicken run this is, of course,
unnecessary, but if you don't have one an
automatic door will relieve you of the burden
of having to open and close it every morning
and evening.

Make sure your guests always have
enough fresh water and food (seeds and
greens). Clean the feeder and waterer
regularly. If you have time, clean the
henhouse daily or at least once a week,
renewing or adding straw to the litter and
replacing dirty straw in the nests with fresh
straw.

Instead of laying down a thick layer of
litter every month or every three months,
just scatter a few handfuls of straw around
the run every week. This way, the litter will
decompose progressively and more evenly.

In rainy weather, a thick layer of straw packed down by active hens becomes the perfect environment for anaerobic decomposition, which generates bad odors (good organic decomposition has almost no odor apart from a slight smell of forest humus). Twice a year—once in January or February before the start of the gardening season and once in October—remove the litter (which is now manure) from the chicken run.

Put your hay, straw, or manure somewhere where your hens have access to it for a few days before using it in your garden. Your mulch will be loosened up and enriched from the chicken droppings!

Rabbits

At one time, rabbit hutches were a common sight on most farms, and like chickens, rabbits were an important part of food self-sufficiency in rural communities. They only need wild grass, vegetables, and a few leafstalks or peelings from the garden, so they are easy to feed—but think twice before getting one!

Unlike hens, which provide eggs, rabbits are only raised for their meat. If you are interested in helping preserve at-risk rabbit breeds, even on a small scale, consider raising heritage breeds like the American, American Chinchilla, Belgian Hare, Blanc de Hotot, Silver, or Silver Fox. According to the FAO (Food and Agriculture Organization of the United Nations) and the UN Environment Program, one-third of domestic breeds around the world are headed for extinction.

8 BEEKEEPING

Honey is a sweetener with many health benefits. It is harvested in summer and can be kept in jars for several years. While the garden keeps you busy in spring and fall, beehives will demand your attention the most in summer during honey harvest and extraction, and in winter when it's time to repair unused hives, clean honey supers, and build new frames. This may sound straightforward, but raising bees is nevertheless complex and requires both specialized knowledge and a significant amount of general know-how.

A fascinating and complex universe

Just because you're an experienced gardener doesn't necessarily mean you'll be a good beekeeper! Unless you take the time to learn a little about the unique and captivating world of bees . . . In this case, a relationship with a friendly and seasoned beekeeper is worth its weight in gold. Spend time with them out in the field for at least a year. Watch them work, listen to their explanations. When the time comes, they'll be able to give you your first swarm, help you install your hives, and offer advice on how to handle the many small disappointments that assail first-time beekeepers.

Bees produce honey all summer long.

Getting started . . .

In the United States, beekeeping regulations vary by state, Check online or talk to your local beekeepers' guild or association to find out what the rules are. A local beekeepers guild may also be able to help you find used equipment.

The beekeeper's calendar

Timing will vary based on where you live. Obviously, seasons are going to be different in New England than in Texas! A quick search online will guide you to beekeeping resources specific to your area, but what follows is a sample calendar suited to most of the northern or middle United States where winters are long and cold. But even within this region, there are variations. Again, you'll find it helpful to talk to members of a local beekeepers guild or even a neighbor with bees to find out what makes most sense for your particular location.

Winter

If you're ordering bees, January is a good time to do so.

In winter, bee colonies slow down. Take advantage of this time to do little jobs that will make your work easier come spring: build your hive frames, tighten the wires that will support the wax foundation, and use a blowtorch to disinfect old hives and honey supers. The first flights will usually begin in February. On a nice sunny day, clean around the hives and sweep the hive stands and landing boards.

Take advantage of the winter months to install wax foundation in the frames you will use in your honey supers when spring comes.

Spring

The first warm spring days are when nectar collection begins. Choose a sunny March day to open each hive and verify how much and how regularly the bees are laying, but don't disturb the colonies more than you have to. Replace any old unused comb with new comb. One-third of the comb in your frames will have to be replaced every year.

Once the bees start collecting nectar, everything takes off. In April, check how much honey is on the frames. Whenever they're full, you can install your first honey supers. In May, the swarms leave the hives to form new colonies: pay attention when this happens and try to recapture the swarms each time if you can. If necessary, bolster a weak hive or one that has lost bees to swarming by replacing one or two almost empty frames with frames filled with brood from a very active hive.

A populous and active colony ensures a bountiful honey harvest.

Summer

Starting in June, monitor your honey supers as they fill. If they are full, and if flowers are still in bloom and bee activity has remained the same, add new honey supers to increase your colonies' storage capacity. Otherwise— after an early heat wave or a dry spring, for example—make sure the frames are fully capped and remove them to extract the honey.

ESSENTIAL BEEKEEPING EQUIPMENT

Beekeeping equipment is obviously highly specialized: you will need hives with frames—opt for the most widely used model in your area, typically either Langstroth or Dadant—honey supers, sheets of beeswax foundation made for frames, a beekeeping jacket with a hat and veil, gloves, a few must-have tools (smoker, brush, and hive tool), an extractor for harvesting honey, and jars to store it in.

A honey super's weight will tell you how much honey is in it.

In a normal year, July is the big month for honey harvesting, especially if you are only planning one harvest. Don't wait too long to do it because the bees need time to refill their honey stores before winter with nectar from fall flowers. Start by setting up your extraction equipment—centrifugal honey extractor, uncapping knife and tray, honey tank, bucket and sponge—in an enclosed space with access to water. To harvest honey from two or three hives, a tidied kitchen will do just fine.

Now you're ready to remove the frames from the hives.

Pull the frames out of the honey super . . .

1 Place an empty honey super on a hive barrow and approach the hives.

2. Light your smoker and puff smoke around the hive entrance.

3. Remove the top and the inner cover, if you have one.

4. Quickly and carefully loosen the frame using your hive tool as a lever.

5. Lift up the frame to see if it is capped. If this is not the case, carefully put it back in place (uncapped honey will ferment).

6. If the frame is uniformly capped, use the brush to gently remove any bees walking around on it and then place the frame in the empty honey super.

7. Move on to the next frame and do the same thing until the honey super in the hive is empty.

8. Remove the now empty honey super and close the hive.

9. Place the frames full of honey near the extractor.

. . . and remove any bees on them using a brush.

Now you can start extracting honey. Uncap the front and back of as many frames as your extractor can fit and then place them in the extractor. Crank the handle, slowly at first then faster and faster. Once one side of each frame is empty, turn them over and repeat the process to extract honey from the other side. The honey drips slowly through a filter into the honey tank via a valve at the base of the extractor. Place the empty frames in the uncapping tray and crush any remaining caps to collect the last of the honey. To prevent

The frame filled with honey is placed in the extractor after being uncapped . . .

. . . and the honey is collected in the honey tank before it is put in jars.

other bee colonies from "stealing" the last traces of honey, clean your extraction equipment thoroughly and put it away when you have finished using it. Store the harvested honey in the tank for a few days, then skim off any small particles on the surface and fill your glass jars. You can store the honey just like that until you are ready to eat it.

After the harvest is over, put away the honey supers in storage. If you need to treat your beehives for *Varroa* mites—tiny parasitic arachnids that are very harmful to bees—think about asking for advice from your local agriculture extension office.

Polyfloral honey

Two or three backyard hives will give you polyfloral honey whose flavor will vary from year to year depending on the spring weather. Beekeepers who harvest monofloral honeys—rapeseed, acacia, lavender, sunflower, etc.—have to move their hives around in order to follow the various blooms. Each time the hives are repositioned, honey is extracted from the comb and labeled.

Fall

In the event of a dry or rainy fall—in both cases, there are fewer flowers, and less nectar is harvested—feed the bee colonies twice with 1 quart (1 liter) of syrup made from equal parts water and sugar. Allow for a one-week interval between each feeding. In October, make sure the bees have enough honey to get them through the winter. If the reserves for each hive are less than 33 pounds (15 kg), feed the colonies again with a syrup that is two-thirds sugar, one-third water. The last nectar will be gathered in November, weather permitting. Once the first cold days arrive, place a protective screen over the hive entrance to keep out small rodents.

Pollen, propolis, and wax

Honey is the main product harvested from a hive, but with a little experience and the right equipment, you can also harvest pollen and propolis (see photo above). You can render beeswax from emptied honeycomb by loading it into a solar wax melter. Use this wax to make candles, furniture polish, or to prepare new frames for next year's harvest.

Feeding your hive a sugar cake will help the bees replenish their winter honey reserves.

Kenya top-bar hives

Unlike traditional hive models that expand vertically as honey supers are stacked on top of the body of the hive, the Kenya top-bar hive is horizontal. This gives the bees plenty of room inside the hive and allows the amount of space for each colony to be adjusted as needed.

A hive that's not quite like the rest . . .

The design of a top-bar hive is relatively simple and usually consists of a wooden box around 3 feet (1 meter) long that is shaped like an inverted trapezoid. Its sides form a 120° angle with the bottom board, which happens to be the same angle bees use when building their honeycomb cells.

The hive body usually measures 9.5–12 inches (24–30 cm) in height and 16 inches (40 cm) in width. The amount of space the bees can occupy is dictated by a divider board that the beekeeper moves along the hive like a cursor as the colony expands. The bottom board is often partially screened, and the roof that protects the hive from bad weather can be flat

or gabled. The whole hive is mounted on legs to make it easier for the beekeeper to tend it.

. . . but it works just as well!

Depending on the model, top-bar hives have a single entrance at one end or multiple entrance holes along the side that can be partially sealed if needed. There are no frames filled with wax foundation, and instead the beekeeper works with around thirty removable wooden bars 1.5 inches wide (35 mm). The bees will attach their honeycomb to these bars. To make the bees' job easier, many beekeepers attach a piece of wood or wax to each bar. When the bees are first introduced to the hive, they are installed at one end and given access to six or eight bars. Later, sliding the divider board down the hive will allow you to add new bars next to the brood as the colony develops. To harvest, just remove the bars with honeycomb on them.
Approved by beginner beekeepers

Beginners appreciate the Kenya top-bar hive because it doesn't require a lot of up-front investment. It is made entirely of wood and anyone with even a basic skill level can build one themselves using plans and tutorials found online. You also won't need to purchase very much equipment—a hive tool, a smoker, and protective gear are all you need. While experienced beekeepers complain that it is too time-consuming to maintain and not as "productive" as the more commonly used hives, it is still an affordable alternative for a beginner beekeeper interested in harvesting honey for personal consumption from two or three hives.

9
GRAIN PRODUCTION

Harvesting grain is traditionally more of a farmer's job than a gardener's. If, however, you have a large piece of land, you can certainly set aside a few hundred square yards to grow some of your own. Grain is a source of food for both animals and humans—bread was our ancestors' primary source of calories—and its byproduct is straw, which, as we have seen, is incredibly important in a self-sufficient garden.

Should I grow grain?

This is a question you need to ask yourself! Before making your decision, know that grains need a relatively large amount of space to grow. Even though cultivating them is fairly simple—they are all direct-seeded—harvesting them without machines is a lot of work. Whatever you decide, do not plant grain if it means sacrificing space for growing vegetables: the yields are not worth it and it will hardly make you more self-sufficient! 120 square yards of wheat will give you

between 90 and 130 pounds (40 and 60 kg) of harvested grain. Planting that same amount of land with potatoes, depending on the variety and weather conditions, will yield between 900 and 1,500 pounds (400 and 700 kg) of tubers for around six hundred planted tubers. There's no comparison!

Corn is the easiest grain to grow in the garden.

Fall planting . . .

Wheat (soft, hard, and spelt), rye, triticale (a wheat-rye hybrid), and winter barley are planted in fall and harvested the following summer. The decision of when to plant grain seed is an important one: sow too early and you risk having weeds or fall parasites invade your grains. Sow too late and the young sprouts are more sensitive to the cold. To find out exactly when you should sow, local farmers (organic or not) are always good people to ask.

. . . and spring planting

Corn, barley, and spring oats are planted between early March and May and are harvested between the end of summer and fall. These grains mature quickly, but their production potential—with the exception of corn—is lower than that of winter grains.

Hard wheat is used to make pasta . . .

. . . and soft wheat allows us to make cakes and bread.

CROP ROTATION—VEGETABLES AND GRAINS

Growing grains improves soil structure and, thanks to grain crops' dense canopies and narrow rows, it also limits weed growth. If you have enough room, "flip" your grain and vegetable zones to optimize the benefits each one brings to the other: softer and more stable soil, increased fertility, and protection from parasites.

→ PLANTING AND HARVEST CALENDAR FOR COMMON GRAINS

Grains	J	F	M	A	M	J	J	A	S	O	N	D
Barley							█			█		
Corn				█	█					█		
Oats			█					█				
Rye							█			█		
Spelt							█			█		
Triticale							█			█		
Wheat, soft							█			█		

█ Planting
█ Harvest

Pseudograins

Millet (pictured) and sorghum are perfect for family gardening because they are easy to grow. Like quinoa and buckwheat, they are not really grains—we call them pseudograins—but they grow in a similar fashion. They are all planted in the spring and are harvested in the four to six months that follow. Like traditional grains, pseudograin seeds are harvested for human and animal consumption. Since they do not contain gluten, their flours are not suitable for breadmaking (unless, of course, you're following a recipe for gluten-free bread), but if mixed with wheat and rye flours they can be used to make a variety of specialty breads.

How to plant grain seed

The traditional method of broadcasting seeds is still used on small parcels of land and especially for pseudograins with small seeds like sorghum, millet, buckwheat, and quinoa. Row planting is a must for grains with very large seeds like corn, and it is also the easiest way to plant wheat, rye, barley, and oats on large areas of land. Place the seeds .75 inches (2 cm) deep in the ground to encourage tillering, or branching out, from the initial seedling. Leave 4 to 6 inches (10 to 15 cm) of space between rows of wheat, rye, barley, or oats, and 20 inches (50 cm) for corn and sorghum. Using an automatic seeder will save you time and help you maintain the proper seeding rate. You don't need to water these plantings unless the weather is extremely dry.

→ SEEDING RATES FOR COMMON GRAINS

Grain	Seeding rate
Barley	110 to 130 lbs/acre (1 to 1.2 kg/are)
Corn	75,000 seeds/acre (1,500 seeds/are)
Oats	110 lbs/acre (1 kg/are)
Rye	88 to 110 lbs/acre (0.8 to 1 kg/are)
Soft wheat (common wheat)	110 to 130 lbs/acre (1 to 1.2 kg/are)
Spelt	110 to 130 lbs/acre (1 to 1.2 kg/are)
Triticale	88 to 110 lbs/acre (0.8 to 1 kg/are)

PLANTING SEEDS FROM HARVESTED GRAINS

Saving grain seed is easy to do. Wheat, spelt, oats, triticale, and barley are self-pollinating. In practice, all you have to do is collect the seeds you need from the annual harvest. There is a risk of cross-pollination—mostly for rye and corn—so consider only growing one variety.

Broadcasting seeds works well for small fields.

Harvesting, storing, and using grains

Choosing when to harvest your grains is not always easy, especially since the timing may vary from one year to the next depending on weather conditions. Grain should be harvested when the stalk is dry and the grains inside the seed-heads of the plant are mature. The plants are either mowed or threshed by hand to separate the grains from the stalks and winnowed to remove the husk and various impurities from the edible grain. In small gardens, picking and cleaning the grains is done manually whereas larger parcels require machinery.

The wonderful thing about grains is that they can be stored for long periods of time. If they are kept dry and away from rodents, they can easily last until the following year, and even as long as several years. Different grains are used for different things, but all of them can be used alone or in combination to feed humans and animals.

Hens eat just about everything, but they especially enjoy grains, which form the foundation of their diet.

→ COOKING WITH GRAINS

Common grains	Uses in the kitchen
Barley	Beer and fermented drinks
Corn	Cornbread, Johnny cakes, and galettes
Millet	Porridge, galettes, and bread
Oats	Vegetable soups, cookies, cakes, oatmeal
Rye	Bread and cakes
Soft wheat and spelt	Bread, cookies, cakes
Sorghum	Cookies, galettes, beignets, and soups
Triticale	Bread, pasta, crêpes, tarts, cakes

→ GRAINS FOR CHICKENS

Common grains	Chicken feed ratio
Barley	Up to 10%
Corn	Up to 40% (seeds, preferably crushed)
Millet	Up to 30%
Oats	No more than 5%
Rye	No more than 5%
Soft wheat and spelt	Up to 20%
Sorghum	No more than 5%
Triticale	No more than 5%

Protein crops

These Fabaceae plants got their name because of the high levels of protein they contain. Among them are peas, fava beans, and lupines, all of which can be grown in rotation with grains. In addition to being a source of chicken feed, they are also attractive in a gardening context because of their ability to naturally fix nitrogen in the air.

10 HARVEST

If you're aiming for food self-sufficiency, your garden will need to provide you with vegetables, herbs, and fruit from January to December. All year long, variety is the general rule: nothing is more boring than eating a meal just like the one you ate yesterday when you know you will also eat the same thing tomorrow. Every season has its own vegetables, herbs, and fruit: I'm sure very few of us can imagine picking strawberries, melons, or tomatoes in winter, for example, but that is precisely when vegetables like mâche, spinach, and Savoy cabbage are harvested. These crops do not like heat or dry weather, so growing them out of season would be difficult and costly.

Spring harvests

In spite of the feverish level of activity that reigns in the garden this time of year, most of your vegetables, herbs, and fruit will not be at your disposal just yet. Less hardy winter vegetables that spent winter in the ground are usually frozen (though mild winters have often made escarole, frisée, Napa cabbage, and chard available until April), and those that better resist the cold like leeks, mâche, and Brussels sprouts are reaching the end of their growing season. On top of that, the first spring plantings—radishes, purple top Milan turnips, and fava beans—are not yet ready to harvest and won't be until the end of spring (April and May). Whatever you have in your garden, keep in mind that the winter and spring weather conditions will have an enormous influence on the availability of vegetables, herbs, and fruit between March and June.

Fresh vegetables available in spring	Herbs available in spring	Fruits available in spring
Artichoke, asparagus, chard, carrot, radicchio, wild chicory, Brussels sprouts, kale, Savoy cabbage, red Russian kale, Asian cabbages, miner's lettuce, zucchini and pattypan squash, spinach, fava beans, cutting lettuce, spring head lettuce, winter head lettuce, purple top Milan turnips, cipollini onion, sorrel, parsnip, pea, dandelion, leek, spring radish, arugula, Jerusalem artichoke	Dill, spring onion, chives, cilantro, tarragon, bay leaf, lovage, curly-leaf parsley, flat-leaf parsley, rosemary, sage, lemon thyme, common thyme	Strawberry, rhubarb

SEASONAL COOKING

A garden filled with vegetables, herbs, and fruits that change with the seasons is sure to stimulate creativity in the kitchen. Spring, for instance, is the season of quiches and savory pies with salads, and summer is the time for barbecues, roasted tomatoes, and crudités. Fall pairs warm and cold dishes together again, and winter is a season of soups and warm cooked meals. Whatever the time of year, just let your imagination be your guide: if you use seasonal ingredients together, it's almost always sure to be good.

Peas are harvested by hand . . .

Summer harvests

Everything changes in the month of April. The last of the spring vegetables are still hanging around the garden and summer crops are bearing their first fruits. Many herbs are at their peak. In July and August, when tomatoes, eggplants, peppers, zucchini, and cucumbers ripen, the garden harvest reaches its culmination. With its seemingly endless series of fruit harvests, the orchard is just as busy.

. . . and lemon verbena is harvested with shears.

Fresh vegetables available in summer	Herbs available in summer	Fruits available in summer
Artichoke, eggplant, chard, red beet, Calabrese broccoli, carrot, kohlrabi, celery, summer frisée, summer escarole, pointed cabbage, summer cauliflower, cucumber, zucchini and pattypan squash, fennel, bush beans, pole beans, summer head lettuce, cutting lettuce, sweet corn, melon and watermelon, onion, sweet potato, peas, pepper, potato, summer purslane, summer radish, arugula, tomato	Garlic, dill, basil, chives, cilantro, gherkin, shallot, tarragon, bay leaf, lovage, lemon balm, mint, oregano, curly-leaf parsley, flat-leaf parsley, chili pepper, rosemary, sage, stevia, lemon thyme, thyme, lemon verbena	Apricot, shadbush, cherry, fig, strawberry, raspberry, red currant, gooseberry, blackberry, peach, summer pear, summer apple, plum, grapes

Fall harvests

Many summer fruiting vegetables tend to stick around the garden until early fall, just when the first fall vegetables are ready to be harvested. If you plant seeds regularly and transplant between March and October, lettuce will be available in your garden non-stop through November and beyond. The first endives of the season can be harvested in early November if they have been force-grown indoors beginning in September or October, and there is such a wide selection of fall fruit varieties that you're sure to have an abundant harvest until mid-October when the cold temperatures arrive. Leaf vegetables, fruiting vegetables, and root vegetables all find their place in the garden between September and November—in fact, the range of crops available in fall rivals that of a summer garden!

Fresh vegetables available in fall	Herbs available in fall	Fruits available in fall
Artichoke, eggplant, chard, red beet, Calabrese broccoli, carrot, celery, celery root, summer and fall frisée, radicchio, wild chicory, summer and fall escarole, Brussels sprouts, head cabbage, kale, fall cauliflower, red cabbage, red Russian kale, bok choy, Napa cabbage, kohlrabi, Asian cabbages, cucumber, Physalis peruviana, butternut squash, turban squash, red kuri squash, pumpkin, zucchini and pattypan squash, endive, spinach, fennel, bush beans, pole beans, fall head lettuce, cutting lettuce, lentil, mâche, fall turnip, sorrel, parsnip, sweet potato, leek, chickpea, pepper, potato, fall and winter radish, arugula, rutabaga, tomato, Jerusalem artichoke	Basil, spring onion, chives, cilantro, tarragon, bay leaf, lovage, lemon balm, mint, oregano, curly-leaf parsley, flat-leaf parsley, chili pepper, rosemary, sage, stevia, lemon thyme, thyme, lemon verbena	Almond, quince, fig, strawberry (climbing varieties), raspberry (climbing varieties), hardy kiwi, kiwi, hazelnut, peach, pear, apple, plum, grape

Almonds are harvested in the fall and make a great snack all winter long.

Napa cabbages are harvested until the first heavy frosts.

Winter harvests

Cold-hardy crops like Brussels sprouts, Savoy cabbage, kale, leeks, spinach, mâche, parsnip, and hardy radicchio varieties can be left in the ground to be harvested even in a very cold winter. Less hardy vegetables like chard, celery, miner's lettuce, frisée, escarole, and rutabaga are harvested until the first severe frosts below 18°F (-8°C). Protected by a row cover or a layer of straw, winter carrots can be pulled up until April or May as needed, and parsley that is transplanted in late summer can be harvested all winter until it goes to seed in late spring.

Fresh vegetables available in winter	Herbs available in winter
Chard, carrot, celery, radicchio, wild chicory, Brussels sprouts, kale, Savoy cabbage, Napa cabbage, miner's lettuce, endive, spinach, mâche, sorrel, parsnip, leek, rutabaga, Jerusalem artichoke	Bay leaf, curly-leaf parsley, flat-leaf parsley, rosemary, sage, lemon thyme, thyme

11
STORING AND PRESERVING YOUR HARVEST

Storing and preserving your vegetables, herbs, and fruit is just as important as harvesting them! You can eat winter squash and less hardy root vegetables all winter long if you store them somewhere safe from frost. Freezing and canning are other ways to preserve your excess summer and fall crops so you can enjoy them until the first harvests the following year.

Root cellars

Potatoes, celery root, red beets, turnips, and winter radishes are pulled up before the first frost and protected from freezing temperatures in basement or hole-in-the-ground root cellars. Any kind of unheated storage space that is frost proof or a cool, well-ventilated basement is perfect for storing pumpkins, red kuri squash, turban squash, butternut squash, and other winter squash.

Fruiting vegetables to store in a basement root cellar	Root vegetables to store in a basement or hole-in-the-ground root cellar
Winter squash (including butternut), turban squash, red kuri squash, and pumpkin	Red beet, carrot, celery root, fall turnip, sweet potato, potato, winter radish, rutabaga

Cold storage

If you harvest them at maturity, legumes, grains, pseudograins, and protein crops can be stored for at least a year in an attic or unheated room. Garlic, shallots, and onions will keep for several months under similar conditions (the storage life varies slightly depending on the variety). Cold storage in a pantry or unheated bedroom is also a good alternative for winter squash if your basement root cellar is cold and damp. Grains (corn in particular) can withstand low temperatures as well, but only if the storage area is completely dry. Unlike other frost-sensitive root vegetables, sweet potatoes actually fare better when kept at room temperature (64°F to 72°F [18°C to 22°C]) instead of somewhere on the cooler side.

Red kuri squash, pumpkins, and winter squash should be stored at 50°F–64°F (10°C–18°C).

Cold storage crops
Beans
Chickpea
Chili pepper
Field pea and split pea
Garlic
Grains: wheat, oats, barley, rye, triticale, millet, sorghum, and corn
Lentil
Onion
Protein crops: fava bean and lupine
Pseudograins: quinoa and buckwheat
Shallot
Turban squash, red kuri squash, pumpkin
Winter squash, including butternut

Excess summer crops can last several months in sterilized jars.

Canning

In this food preservation method, glass jars fitted with rubber rings are filled with vegetables or fruit and covered with sweetened or salted water before being plunged into boiling water for 30 to 45 minutes. The heat destroys active bacteria and allows you to preserve your freshly picked foods for several months, typically until the following year's harvest. You can can most vegetables on their own, as part of a mixture of diced vegetables, or as whole meals. Refer to the National Center for Home Food Preservation's website for more specific canning guidelines.

Vegetables to can	Fruits to can
Eggplant, chard, red beet, cardoon, carrot, celery, celery root, all cabbage family members, zucchini, fennel, bush and pole beans, sweet corn, leek, peas, pepper, salsify, scorzonera, tomato	Apricot, cherry, quince, fig, peach, pear, plum

Freezing

Freezing is a practical preservation method that works for most foods, but because the freezer consumes so much energy, it should only be used for items that cannot be preserved by more traditional means. So, as easy as it is, freezing carrots, spinach, sorrel, parsnip, leek, squash, red beets, and turnip simply isn't justifiable. The same is true for parsley, which overwinters easily in the garden under a basic row cover.

PRESERVING HERBS

Herbs are difficult to preserve and tend to lose a lot of their flavor. The most effective way—though it is a kind of last resort—is to finely chop your herbs after washing and then put them in an ice cube tray. Once frozen, place the cubes in a freezer bag and return them to the freezer. You can take them out to cook with whenever you need to!

Vegetables to freeze	Herbs to freeze	Fruit to freeze
Artichoke (heart), asparagus, eggplant, all members of the cabbage family, zucchini and pattypan squash, fennel, fava bean, bush bean, pole bean, peas, pepper, tomato	Dill, basil, chives, tarragon, lovage, parsley	Apricot, black currant, cherry, fig, strawberry, raspberry, red currant, gooseberry, kiwi, melon, blackberry, blueberry, peach, plum

Preservation method or just plain good?

Making jam, a mixture of fruit and sugar that is cooked to prevent fermentation and kill bacteria, is a tasty way to preserve an overabundance of summer fruit.

Other food preservation techniques

When it comes to preserving food, human beings have quite the imagination. The flavors in many foods can be preserved and even improved when stored in oil, vinegar, salt, or alcohol, or if those foods are smoked, dried, or lactofermented. Depending on your tastes and the equipment and time you have available, perhaps you could give some of these traditional preservation methods a try.

HERBAL TEA PLANTS

Fragrant herbs like hyssop, mint, lavender, rosemary, sage, and thyme can keep for several years if they are picked right before the flowers have bloomed or immediately after. To dry them, place the herbs in perforated wooden crates in a dark room at room temperature for a few days.

Oil, vinegar, and brine can add variety to your winter canned foods.

12

GARDEN CALENDAR FOR A SELF-SUFFICIENT YEAR

In a self-sufficient garden, the real limiting factor is the time you have and how you use it. Whatever tasks are on your to-do list, make sure you do them at the right time of year. You could plant a potted tree in the summer, but what's the point? You'll have to monitor it extremely carefully to be sure it's getting enough water, and weed it constantly, but you can easily plant the same tree with bare roots in October or November with none of the hassle. Once the tree is in the ground, you won't have to take care of it anymore and can move on to something else. In the garden, going against the seasons is never productive. If you prioritize efficiency and planning, you'll be well on your way to food independence.

Garden 10 minutes/ 120 square yards/day

Planting a garden certainly requires work, but most of all it requires availability: you must be there when your garden needs you. This is especially true when it comes to tending your chickens and beehives! You will of course be more in demand in spring than in winter, but when you find your rhythm—the first two or three years will take up even more time—you can plan on an average of 10 minutes of work per 120 square yards per day.

Why your garden needs you all year long . . .

Anyone can garden in April or May! And, yes, those two months are a critical time for a self-sufficient garden. But the work doesn't end there: as we have seen, harvesting continues uninterrupted from January to December. Each season has its own set of tasks to be done.

Winter

Early winter is the time to put in place everything that will protect your garden against the coming bad weather (insulate the greenhouse and henhouse, cover less hardy vegetables or move them to a shelter, make a plan to keep water lines from freezing, etc.). Once winter is in full swing, start preparing for spring. In fact, anticipating all of the work ahead of you will help you avoid a bottleneck when the season kicks off in April or May.

→ TIME FOR . . .

- General maintenance
- Vegetable cultivation
- Herb cultivation
- Fruit cultivation
- Grain cultivation
- Henhouse maintenance
- Beehive maintenance

The dates listed may vary depending on the region and annual weather conditions.

Task	J	F	M	A	M	J	J	A	S	O	N	D
Remove any remnants of old plantings, aerate the soil, and spread compost and composted manure.	■	■	■								■	■
Winterproof water lines and insulate the greenhouse and henhouse, if necessary.	■	■									■	■
Check seed supply, test germinative potential as needed, and plan the growing season.	■	■										■
Harvest as needed the hardy vegetables that have been left in the ground and regularly inspect the vegetables in the root cellar.	■	■									■	■
Force Belgian endive, dandelion, and wild chicory in a dark cellar.	■	■									■	■
Prune any pome fruit trees.	■	■									■	■
Protect rosemary, tarragon, and bay leaf from the cold.	■	■									■	■
Repair the honey supers and frames needed for the spring.	■	■									■	■
Make sure the hens have plenty of water and grains.	■	■									■	■

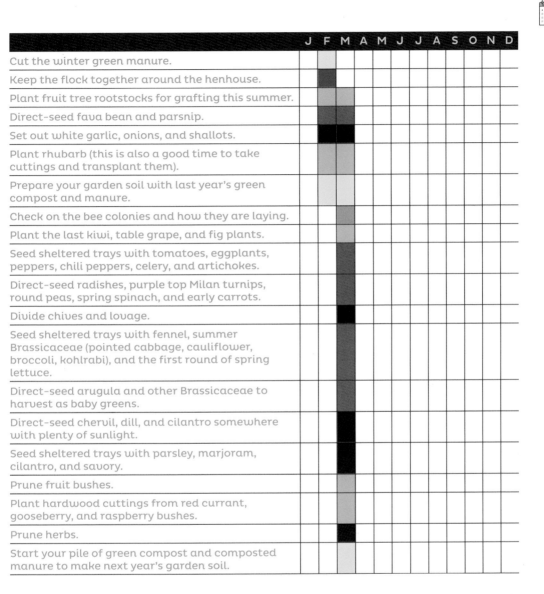

	J	F	M	A	M	J	J	A	S	O	N	D
Cut the winter green manure.		▓										
Keep the flock together around the henhouse.		▓										
Plant fruit tree rootstocks for grafting this summer.		▓	▓									
Direct-seed fava bean and parsnip.		▓	▓									
Set out white garlic, onions, and shallots.		▓	▓									
Plant rhubarb (this is also a good time to take cuttings and transplant them).		▓										
Prepare your garden soil with last year's green compost and manure.		▓										
Check on the bee colonies and how they are laying.			▓									
Plant the last kiwi, table grape, and fig plants.			▓									
Seed sheltered trays with tomatoes, eggplants, peppers, chili peppers, celery, and artichokes.			▓									
Direct-seed radishes, purple top Milan turnips, round peas, spring spinach, and early carrots.			▓									
Divide chives and lovage.			▓									
Seed sheltered trays with fennel, summer Brassicaceae (pointed cabbage, cauliflower, broccoli, kohlrabi), and the first round of spring lettuce.			▓									
Direct-seed arugula and other Brassicaceae to harvest as baby greens.			▓									
Direct-seed chervil, dill, and cilantro somewhere with plenty of sunlight.			▓									
Seed sheltered trays with parsley, marjoram, cilantro, and savory.			▓									
Prune fruit bushes.			▓									
Plant hardwood cuttings from red currant, gooseberry, and raspberry bushes.			▓									
Prune herbs.			▓									
Start your pile of green compost and composted manure to make next year's garden soil.			▓									

Spring

As winter slides gradually into spring, start planting seeds for your greenhouse and outdoor crops. After that, your garden will keep you busy until May. Work during these three months—March, April, and May—is what the coming summer harvest will depend on.

→ TIME FOR . . .

- General maintenance
- Vegetable cultivation
- Herb cultivation
- Fruit cultivation
- Grain cultivation
- Henhouse maintenance
- Beehive maintenance

The dates listed may vary depending on the region and annual weather conditions.

	J	F	M	A	M	J	J	A	S	O	N	D
Transplant the first spring lettuce seedlings.			■									
Plant leek seeds in trays.			■									
Plant seed-producing onion plants.			■									
Sow oats.			■									
Plant fig trees, grapevines, kiwi trees, and any other fruit bushes that could not be planted in fall.			■	■								
Direct-seed seasonal carrots and peas.			■	■								
Bleach dandelions outdoors.			■									
Continue bleaching Belgian endives, dandelion, and wild chicory in a basement or cellar.			■	■								
Somewhere indoors, repot the tomato, eggplant, pepper, chili pepper, and artichoke seedlings you started last month.				■								
Seed sheltered trays with zucchini, squash, cucumber, and melon seeds (repot two or three weeks after planting).				■								
Seed trays with fall Brassicaceae (cauliflower, red cabbage, head cabbage).				■								

← Since they have almost identical growing needs, tomato and basil can be planted together at the same time.

	J	F	M	A	M	J	J	A	S	O	N	D
Plant early and midseason potatoes.				■								
Seed sheltered trays with basil.				■								
Plant sage, lemon verbena, stevia, and any herb cuttings from last summer.				■								
Plant summer Brassicaceae and artichokes in the garden.				■								
Seed sheltered trays with summer escarole and frisée.				■								
Plant asparagus crowns.				■								
Transplant spring pink garlic.				■								
Transplant celery in trays with large cells.				■								
Check the level of honey in the hives and place honey supers if needed.				■								
Sow the second round of spring lettuce seed and plant the seedlings that were started in March.				■	■							
Cut back artichoke plants.				■	■							
Plant corn.				■	■							
Water and weed as needed.				■	■	■	■	■	■			
Chicks and ducklings hatch.				■	■							
First direct-seeding for chervil, dill, and cilantro.				■	■							
Harvest spring vegetables, herbs, and fruit.				■	■							
Transplant the curly chervil, cilantro, savory, and any aromatic seedlings you started in early spring.					■							
Monitor swarming and recapture swarms as needed.					■							
Transplant the Solanaceae and Cucurbitaceae seedlings that were started in March and April in the garden.					■							
Second round of planting kohlrabi seeds.					■							
Plant winter Brassicaceae seeds (Brussels sprouts, Savoy cabbage, kale).					■							
Transplant fall Brassicaceae.					■							

	J	F	M	A	M	J	J	A	S	O	N	D
First round of planting filet and mangetout bush bean seeds.					X							
Transplant leeks in the garden.					X							
Second tray seeding for parsley.					X							
Transplant basil in the garden.					X	X						
Hand pollinate or set up isolation cages for cross-pollinating crops.					X	X						
Transplant celery in the garden.					X	X						
Sow third round of lettuce seed and transplant the seedlings that were started in April.					X	X						
Transplant summer escarole and frisée in the garden.					X	X						
Seed sheltered trays with fall escarole and frisée.					X	X						
Direct-seed red beet and summer radish.					X	X						
Plant storage potatoes.					X	X						
Pinch out Solanaceae and Cucurbitaceae plants as needed.					X	X						
Raise chicks and ducklings.					X	X	X					
Set up summer mulch piles.					X		X	X				
Harvest vegetables, herbs, and fruits as they ripen throughout the season.					X	X	X	X	X			

143

Summer

Mulch your newly planted crops starting in early June. The first grain harvests, particularly if you are growing barley, will provide you with all the straw you need. The previous months' plantings need to be weeded, pinched, and watered. The seeds and seedlings you plant now will be for fall and winter harvests. Sowing perennial herbs, taking cuttings from herb and fruit plants, and grafting fruit trees in the summer will give you young plants next spring. If you'd like to enjoy part of your summer harvest this winter, preserve your extra fruit, vegetables, and herbs by canning, freezing, or drying them. Seeds for future plantings can be harvested as they mature throughout the season.

→ TIME FOR . . .

- General maintenance
- Vegetable cultivation
- Herb cultivation
- Fruit cultivation
- Grain cultivation
- Henhouse maintenance
- Beehive maintenance

The dates listed may vary depending on the region and annual weather conditions.

	J	F	M	A	M	J	J	A	S	O	N	D
Plant winter Brassicaceae and leeks.						■						
Direct-seed storage carrots.						■						
Direct-seed Belgian endives, dandelions, and wild chicory to force this winter.						■						
Direct-seed gherkins.						■						
Seed trays with chives and lovage.						■						
Take cuttings from the following plants: thyme, sage, anise hyssop, hyssop, oregano, lemon balm, rosemary, etc.						■						
Set up stakes for pole beans and then plant the seeds.						■						
Plant shelling bush bean seeds.						■						

← September is the best month for planting strawberry plants.

	J	F	M	A	M	J	J	A	S	O	N	D
Second and most important round of planting filet and mangetout bush bean seeds.						X						
Direct-seed summer radishes.						X						
Take fruit bush cuttings.						X	X					
Transplant the parsley seedlings you started in April.							X					
Plant the fourth round of lettuce seeds and transplant the seedlings you started in May.						X	X					
Prop up any heavy-laden fruit tree branches.							X					
Summer prune fruit trees and bushes as needed.							X					
Harvest summer vegetables, herbs, and fruit.							X					
Prepare summer jams.							X					
Harvest seeds for future plantings as they mature throughout the season.						X	X					
Harvest honey.							X					
Harvest mature soft wheat, spelt, rye, triticale, and barley.							X					
Plant the last round of filet and mangetout bush bean seeds.							X					
Plant the second round of fennel seed.							X					
Plant the third round of kohlrabi seed.							X					
Cut strawberry runners and transplant to trays.							X					
Summer prune early and seasonal peach tree varieties after harvesting the fruit.							X					
Second direct-seeding for chervil, dill, and cilantro.							X					
Transfer the perennial and shrubby aromatic herbs that you planted or cut in June to small pots.							X	X				
Graft pome and stone fruit trees.							X	X				
Harvest and can gherkins.							X	X				
Plant the fifth round of lettuce seed and transplant the seedlings that you started in June.							X	X				
Plant fall escarole and frisée.							X	X				
Seed trays with radicchio and sugarloaf chicory.							X	X				

GARDEN CALENDAR FOR A SELF-SUFFICIENT YEAR

	J	F	M	A	M	J	J	A	S	O	N	D
Direct-seed fall turnips and winter radishes.							■	■				
Transplant the second group of parsley seedlings.							■	■				
Plant fall mâche and spinach seed.							■					
Freeze and can excess crops.								■	■			
Prune raspberry bushes.							■	■				
Sow spring onion seeds.								■				
Seed a third round of trays with parsley.								■				
Plant seeds for fall mâche and fall and winter radishes.								■				
Harvest oats once mature.								■				
Plant winter lettuce seed.								■	■			
Plant the sixth round of lettuce seed and transplant the seedlings you started in July.								■	■			
Transplant radicchio, sugarloaf chicory, and cornet chicory (broad-leaved endive) in the garden.								■	■			
Direct-seed arugula and other Brassicaceae to harvest as young shoots.								■	■			
Make pesto and preserve tomatoes, peppers, and eggplants in oil.								■	■			
Harvest your storage potatoes and keep them somewhere protected from the cold.								■	■			
Repot any fruit bush cuttings taken in previous months.								■	■			
Transplant strawberry plants in the garden.								■	■			

Fall

Pull up any vegetables and herbs that have reached the end of their growing season. If your soil is compact, aerate with a spading fork before covering it with straw or manure, which can be composted but does not have to be. Otherwise, if your soil is loose, you can deposit your organic matter on the ground without tilling it first. Move cold-sensitive fruiting vegetables and fall root vegetables somewhere protected from frost and begin force-growing crops like endive, dandelion, etc. Your final plantings and transplants of the year will become your late fall, winter, and spring harvests.

→ **TIME FOR . . .**

- General maintenance
- Vegetable cultivation
- Herb cultivation
- Fruit cultivation
- Grain cultivation
- Henhouse maintenance
- Beehive maintenance

The dates listed may vary depending on the region and annual weather conditions.

	J	F	M	A	M	J	J	A	S	O	N	D
Direct-seed mâche.									■			
Seed trays with winter lettuce seed.									■			
Transplant the parsley seedlings you started last month.									■			
Transplant the fall lettuce seedlings you started in August.									■			
Feed the bees if their honey stores are low.									■			
Direct-seed root chervil.									■	■		
Plant fall purple garlic and gray shallots.									■	■		
Harvest fall vegetables, herbs, and fruit.									■	■	■	
Harvest storage apples and pears and transfer to root cellar.										■		
Transfer winter squash to root cellar.										■		
Transfer less hardy root vegetables (turnips, red beets, winter radishes, etc.) to root cellar (basement or hole-in-the-ground).										■		

	J	F	M	A	M	J	J	A	S	O	N	D
Last hive check before hibernation.										■		
Sow soft wheat, spelt, rye, triticale, and barley seeds.										■		
Harvest corn.										■		
Transplant winter lettuce seedlings.										■		
Hens born in the spring lay their first eggs.										■	■	
Plant all fruit trees and bushes.										■	■	
Prune stone fruit trees.										■		
Prepare the henhouse for winter and add corn to the feed ration.										■		
Transfer the perennial and shrubby herbs you propagated in June and repotted in late summer to a covered area.	■	■									■	■

Hens will lay fewer and fewer eggs in fall and winter but will never stop completely.

13
PERMACULTURE AND AUTONOMY

Permaculture is perhaps the most well-known technique for achieving a self-sufficient garden. Rather than segregating vegetables and herbs, the chicken coop, fruit trees and bushes, grains, and beehives from each other, it aims to combine all parts of a garden into a cohesive whole in which every element coexists in harmony with the others. This whole also includes the home and the people who live in it and forms a dense interconnected network. The principles of permaculture will help guide your decision-making process and simplify your interventions in the garden.

Using nature as a model

The only energy source a forest or prairie needs is the sun! And they certainly don't require fertilizer, treatments, or tilling. But this doesn't keep them from growing and developing year after year, all the while producing a considerable amount of potentially edible biomass. These ecosystems function so well because they are filled with a wide variety of naturally growing plants that are suited to their location's geography and climate. Seeds are sown and living things reproduce with no intervention from humans, and as a result these systems become entirely self-sustaining. As Leonardo da Vinci once remarked, "Nature alone is the master of true genius," and permaculture follows this same principle: observe the way things happen in nature and act accordingly.

The right way to solve a problem

Whatever issue you're trying to resolve, whether it be a minor detail or a more wide-reaching decision, the approach in permaculture is always the same. First, observation will help give you a clear understanding of the problem. Then, reflection will guide you toward a potential decision. When these steps have been completed, take action that optimizes the situation, deftly maneuvers around obstacles, and maximizes benefits.

Best practices

During the creation of a permaculture garden, the land is organized into several zones in order to make moving around in and tending the garden easier in the future. The tasks a gardener has to do every day are concentrated around the home, and those that require less regular attention are farther away in proportion to the amount of work involved. Five zones following this pattern radiate out from the house (zone 0) in a series of roughly concentric circles:

- Zone 1 consolidates tasks that require the gardener's attention every day, like tending herbs and vegetables.

You may have many different crops, but in spite of this fact—or maybe because of it—it is essential to always keep the whole picture in mind.

• Zone 2 is for food production that only requires significant attention at certain times of year. This includes work in the greenhouse, movable tunnels, the orchard, and high biodiversity hedges.

• The pastures and grains in zone 3 require even less regular attention.

• Zone 4 is where you harvest wood.

• Lastly, zone 5 is a wildlife zone that requires no intervention, much like a wild prairie, lake, or wood.

A garden smaller than 700–800 square yards is primarily structured around the first three zones and zones 4 and 5 are reserved for large or very large pieces of land. But, as always in permaculture, there is plenty of flexibility. One part of the garden may straddle two zones or even three. The chicken run, for example, may extend into the orchard in zone 3 even though the henhouse is in zone 1. Beehives—which don't require much room but do need regular attention and interventions at very specific times throughout the year—can be placed in the transition space between zones 2 and 3. The goal is to achieve maximal results with minimal work: this is the great leitmotif of permaculture.

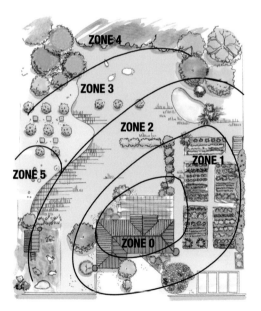

Zone 0—Living area
Zone 1—Vegetable garden
Zone 2—Fruit hedge, chicken coop, orchard
Zone 3—Pastures, grain
Zone 4—Wood harvesting
Zone 5—Wildlife zone

The permaculture garden is structured in five zones.

Whether crops are planted in flat or raised beds, a permaculture garden strives to maximize harvests while limiting interventions.

Simplified interventions

In permaculture, garden work revolves around plantings and harvests. After several years of intensive use of organic matter, the soil naturally softens on its own. Once this happens, working the soil is reduced to a simple aeration now and then, and in the best of cases, no work at all! Whether it is fresh or pre-composted, organic matter should be placed on top of the soil, not buried in it—this limits evaporation (and the amount of watering you'll have to do) all while considerably reducing the need for weeding.

Permaculture also rejects the very notion of waste. Everything—old plant residues, chicken coop litter, branches cut from fruit trees—is reinjected back into the new production cycle.

Let's recap: diversified plantings, a simplified seasonal maintenance plan, and abundant harvests . . . No doubt about it! Whether you're a neophyte or a seasoned gardener, if you're working toward food independence—or independence, period—permaculture is the right tool for the job.

In permaculture, the garden is structured around five zones. →

Index

Photo credits